Successful Real Estate & Property Investment For New investors: how to achieve financial freedom. Revised Edition.

Successful Real Estate & Property Investment For New investors:

how to achieve financial freedom.

Revised Edition.

Why invest in property- the benefits.
How to make money in real estate- gearing and leverage.
Financing your investment. Investing to retire early- wealth creation.
Asset protection.
Legally reduce your tax.
Tax variation and property management.
Understanding property investment and the property market.

Successful Real Estate & Property Investment For New investors: how to achieve financial freedom. Revised Edition.

Successful Real Estate & Property Investment For New investors: how to achieve financial freedom. Revised Edition.

Successful Real Estate & Property Investment For New investors: how to achieve financial freedom. Revised Edition.

How To Make Money From Real Estate & Property Investment:
start replacing your job today.
The benefits of property investment.
Invest using other people's money.
Legally reduce your tax.
How to make money in property.
Living your dream and much more...
Wilnes Radegonde

Successful Real Estate & Property Investment For New investors: how to achieve financial freedom. Revised Edition.

Successful Real Estate & Property Investment For New investors: how to achieve financial freedom. Revised Edition.

Disclaimer:

No part of this book may be reproduced or transmitted in any form or by any means, graphic, electronic, or mechanical, including photocopying, recording, taping, or by any information storage retrieval system, without the permission, in writing, from the publisher.

The material in this book is for purposes of general information only and not intended to be advice. Every effort has been made in compiling the contents of the book. However, no guarantees can be given in relation to the accuracy of the information. The book represents the personal experience of the author who is not a licensed advisor or financial planner.

No reader should rely solely on the information in the book as it is not intended to be the only source of investment advice. All readers are advised to consult independent and qualified advisors and accountants before undertaking investments as each investor's individual circumstance is different. All investments carry risks. The author and publisher cannot accept any responsibility for injury or loss or damage to any reader or person acting or refraining from action as a result of reading material in this book, whether whole or any part of the contents of this publication.

To have a look at my other books visit:
www.xlibris.com.au/Radegonde.html
http://stores.lulu.com/w478040
www.strategicpublishinggroup.com/title/PropertyInvestmentGuideforSuccessfulWealthCreationAndEarlyRetirement.html
www.tiny.cc/321qp

ISBN: 978-1-4461-7708-2

Published by: Lulu.com.

Acknowledgement:

I would like to thank my wife, Yamin, for her support in helping me write this book. I've enjoyed and worked hard to write this second book. I hope that you find the book useful. The story of Margaret Lomas, author and property investor inspired me to invest in property and write this book.

I would also like to thank the two property investor's magazines for allowing me to use their ideas. I'm grateful and full of thanks for the people at The Australian Property Investor's Magazine,Your Mortgage Magazine and Your Investment Property Magazine for giving me permission to use some of the copyright ideas in this book. A special thanks to Lane Boy at the Australian Property Investor Magazine for giving me permission to use the copyright materials in this book.

Editor: Yamin Radegonde.

Successful Real Estate & Property Investment For New investors: how to achieve financial freedom. Revised Edition.

Contents

Introduction

I made the decision four years ago to try property investment for my early retirement. The rental income from my properties and capital growth to-date have been great and rising each year. Within 10 years, I will be able to live off my rental income and capital growth which will provide a higher income than my job as a high school teacher. The best way to secure your financial future is to take the initiative and invest into property rather than putting all your money in superannuation, especially after the financial mismanagement which caused the financial crisis of 2008. Billions of dollars of investor's money were lost in the stock market.

I finally realised in 2004, that teaching is not going to give me the lifestyle I greatly desired. Many people are retiring early due to financial independence that they have achieved by investing in property. This is a dream that can become a reality if you're focused, determined and willing to learn from those people. However, only about 10% of the population will realise this dream. This is because:

1.Very few people take the risk and borrow millions of dollars to invest in property to create wealth for themselves and replace their income from their day job.

2. Many people think it's too hard and don't even try.

3. Others realise that their income cannot support more investments and don't bother to investigate clever ways to borrow more money to buy more investment properties.

There is always a way to get ahead. If many people have become rich and most started from scratch, you can do it too. You need to investigate before giving up. I've always wanted to own my home but didn't think of property investing as a vehicle to achieving financial freedom. I always thought that there must be a way to achieve this but didn't know how to do it. I always thought of the stock market and having a business as the money maker. But I know that the risk is high unless you are very smart and know what you're doing. A lot of businesses fail in the first year alone, and many stock market investors lose billions each year. I've heard of terrible stories of people losing all their life saving and jumping off the windows of their apartments as a result. I've always thought that people make money on the stock market then use it to buy a flash home and a holiday apartment in the city and a holiday home close to the beach.

I came across the power and benefits of property investment early in 2004, when I bought my first property and rented it out for 1 year. I quickly realised how easy it is to get into property investment with little or no money from your own pocket and the power of capital growth. Very few people have the courage to be rich. Many think that they don't have the time or the knowledge and money to invest. I was determined to change that. I will get there, and do whatever it takes to make it happen.

Many people will try to talk you out of borrowing a lot of money to invest in property. Don't be discouraged and scared because this will stop you from ever realising your dream. Today, I have about $1million in debt, but I don't wake up in the middle of the night thinking about it. I plan to double the debt in the next few years without fear. I've acquired the knowledge of how to manage large debts. Good debt means more properties and more equity and wealth. You cannot be wealthy and financially free unless you take risk and get yourself into debt.

Why is property investment important?

- For capital growth to make you wealthy.
- For recurring rental income to service the debt and make you rich.
- For financial freedom.
- To reduce your tax bill while you work and use it to create wealth for yourself.

I've outlined all the benefits of property investment and how I've started on the road to financial freedom. You need to educate yourself and books are the best way to start.

Avoiding costly mistakes.

I've also included all the mistakes I've made and how they've cost me thousands of dollars and slowed down my property accumulation plan. I'll explain all the ways to avoid costly mistakes. I hope you make the most of the advice on property investment. I've done all the research and included all the practical advice that will set you off the road to financial freedom.

What property to buy and how to manage your portfolio?

I will show you how to bargain for good deals, and ways to ensure that you don't shoot yourself in the foot by buying expensive properties and paying too much. It is important to have the property evaluated before you invest or buy. The key to successful property investment is in buying the right property, at the right price and in the right location. I've outlined where to buy and the types of property that delivers the best capital growth and those that provide the best rental returns. It is important to get a qualified property manager to manage your properties and the dangers of managing it yourself.

The tax advantages and how to prepare for tax return.

The tax deductions and benefits that property investors receive are amazing and getting a tax depreciation schedule done on all your investments can put thousands of dollars in your pocket each year. There is a one page form to fill out for this and then fax it to the depreciation specialist. You should receive your professional tax office approved report within 1-4 weeks. I've explained how to prepare for tax returns.

Invest now, don't rely on superannuation.

The majority of people don't invest in the hope that they can rely on a government pension or their superannuation. Retirement laws will change as western societies face an ageing population. There will be more pensioners than workers. Retirement age will increase as the population ages and there is a need for workers to stay in their job longer to support the economy. You will have to work longer before you can to access your superannuation.

So, invest in property now and reap the benefits before you get too old. It is best to retire at around 45-50 years old through property investment and still have the energy and money to live comfortably than waiting to access your superannuation. You have to help yourself, as superannuation payment might not be enough to support you or provide the lifestyle you want.

Why is property investment the best type of investment?

I've heard many people talking negatively about property market and, that it will crash. They say that it is not good to buy now but sell what you have before the market goes down further. This is silly, because those people have no idea what property investment is. The world wealth is based on the property market and the property market like the economy goes up and down. What goes down will eventually come up. The key is for you to prepare yourself to enjoy the ride before the media starts talking about recovery and boom times again. Now is the time to invest providing you also establish a buffer cash reserve (line of credit) for 'a day' and fix your interest rates for at least three years. Demand for house and land will continue and increase as people will still need homes to live in regardless of the state of the economy.

The benefits of property investing.

I've experienced for myself that working hard won't get you anywhere. I'm a high school teacher and realise that working hard will never provide me with the financial freedom I dream of. Unless you invest, you will never be financially free. Even if you work in the mines or own a business and receive a great income, will will never be financial free as the tax office will take about half of that income. When you stop working, your income will stop unless you've invested your spare cash. You have to work very hard but also smart, otherwise you will be wasting your time.

Money management skills.

It is important that you invest wisely and pay off all non-tax deductible debt as soon as possible. You need to appreciate that time is limited. If you have credit cards and personal loans pay off these first as they carry higher interest rates. The sooner you start to deal effectively with your finances the better. The best way is to consolidate all your credit cards into a personal loan as it is about 25% cheaper than credit cards.

You need to learn how to avoid temptations, spending less, save and invest more. If you have a house, consolidate these non-tax deductible loans into your house to reduce your expenses and put you in a good position to invest. When you do invest, first set up interest only repayment for all your loans to maximise your borrowing capacity and use the extra funds to pay off personal debts.

To become financially wealthy you need to manage your hard earned cash and not let your lifestyle control you. I quickly realised that I have to control my personal spending habits and save part of my income for investment.

Property millionaire's mindset.

You need to develop a property millionaire's mindset if you want to succeed as a property investor. I realised that this is the only way you can make it, by taking risks. Due to factors such as upbringing and environment, many people become risk-averse later on in adulthood. You have to break free from this habit and develop a plan of how to become financially free for yourself. You have to start somewhere. I'm sure that you will find the book informative and useful in highlighting the benefits of property investment and the many techniques that you can use to buy and accelerate your property portfolio. Remember like shares, in property investing, you need to buy low (cheaper), the right property and in the right location to reap the full benefits of capital growth and good rental returns. About 90% of property investors only buy one or two properties and 10% buy more than two properties and make serious wealth. To achieve positive cash flow, the rental returns must exceed cash outflow. For educated investors, the best time to buy is when the economy slows down. You then wait until the economy recovers and reaps the results of capital growth.

Investor's tip:
It is important to see a financial planner and an accountant before you start investing to work out the tax entitlements and benefits on your planned investment.

Part 1-
Beginning to invest in property- the benefits.

Chapter 1-
Why is investing in property the best and fastest way to achieve financial freedom?

The advantages of real estate:
I started to invest in property once I realised the tremendous benefits of it and how the rich make their money. **I invest into the property market:**

1. For capital growth to make me wealthy.
2. To use my tax to create wealth for myself.
3. For increasing rental income to service my debt and live off it later on.
4. For financial freedom so that I have the freedom to decide if I want to work or not.

A- Capital growth and wealth creation.
Since the 1950s, house prices in Australia have risen on average by 3% a year after inflation. Between 1995 and 2005, Australian's median house prices rose by about 10% per year. Property market goes through a cycle of boom and slump. Overall the returns offset the downturns and delivers consistent and good returns over the long term. In Western Australia, from the year 2000-2010, property

prices have increased by at least 300%. The average family home which cost just above $100,000 in 2000, today (2010) cost over $300,000. My father-in-law bought a house for $72,000 in 2001. Today, this house is worth over $350,000.

According to research, property prices double every seven to ten years. Now, if you've invested wisely in a $300,000 property in 2009, it will be worth $600,000 or more in 2019. But if you've overpaid for the property, for example, by $50,000, your capital gains will be reduced by $50,000.

My property in Mandurah is now worth over $400,000. This means that I've made over $200,000 in three years, more than my PAYG income of $76,000 per year. My Investment at The Vines which cost me about $305,000 to build in 2007, is now worth just below $400,000. The Caversham's villa which I bought for $260,000, is now worth about $360,000. Overall, I made about $400,000 in capital growth in three years. That's over a $100,000 per year.

B- Long term objective- buy and hold.

When investing in property, you should have a long term view as your overall investment strategy. You need to buy and hold all your properties to benefit from capital growth and increasing equity.

C- To provide rental and passive residual income.

Property investment is good due to the reliability of rental income. You can also claim the cost of maintaining the property while it is vacant but still on the rental market. Better still, over time, your properties will become cash flow positive. You will have excess income that you can use to finance your lifestyle or retirement.

D- Leverage: the ability to borrow a large amount of money to buy more properties.

Leverage is simply putting a small amount of your money and borrowing a larger amount to increase your buying/investing power. This will increase the speed of making money and wealth creation. You can use $200,000 of your equity and gear it by borrowing $800,000. Alternatively, you can put down $100,000 deposit (using your equities) and borrow $1 million dollars to buy more properties.

E- Reduce your tax to help service the loans- tax benefits and deductions.

Real estate has the added advantage, in that you can claim the depreciating building, fittings, fixtures and losses on your property, if you live in the UK, Australia and New Zealand. As the land increases in value, you still continue to claim these deductions year after year, long after you've paid $500 tax-deductible fee to get a professional tax depreciation schedule. As you can see below, the investors have a reason to get up in the morning as they're using their taxes to make thousands of dollars in capital appreciation.

Use your tax deductions to:

- Pay off the loan on your property investments.
- Help you acquire more appreciable assets and create wealth.

Let's see an example of tax deductions on an investment property.

Table 1- Property investment ($300,000). Depreciation benefits of $6,000.

James-accountant		**Paul-accountant**
1 investment		No investment
Income:	$75,000	$75,000
Taxes@20%:	$15,000	$15,000
Real property losses:	$7,000	No property losses
Depreciation benefits:	$6,000	No asset
Net rental loss: $13,000		No property
Tax saving/refunds: @$5,000 (approx)		Very little @$1,000.
Personal contribution: @$2,000+.		

As shown from the table below James has bought an investment and Paul hasn't.

James has one property investment: $300,000 property investment loan, with a $350 per week rent and interest rates fixed at 5.5%. His loan repayment will be about $1,650 per month ($19,800 per year). Assume other maintenance costs of $4,000 per annum. His annual rent will be about $16,800. He has a net rental loss of about $13,000 but a real property loss of about $7,000-$8,000. His total refund will be about $5,000. James' property is appreciating at a rate of, for example, of 3%-5 per year or about $5,000-10,000 and more during boom times.

Investor's tip:
Don't buy for the wrong reasons to pay less tax. Never buy with the intention to get tax deductions and a bigger tax return.

F- You can borrow against it.

I like the idea of being able to borrow against your property. Investing in property will open a whole new world of opportunities for the investor. You will be able to go to the banks and borrow thousands of dollars. Property investment forces you to save money, trim your expenses and become better at managing money.

In time, a well-chosen property will have both capital and rental income growth. Your equity goes up, but debt stays the same (interest only loans). You will then be in a position to buy more properties. Plan to acquire 3-4 properties in the first 5 years. Use the accumulated equity to buy another 2-3 properties in the next 5 years. You need to be patient in your journey, take one step at a time, sacrifice and have a long-term goal. You need to start small and think big.

G- You're in control.

Real estate is a good investment because unlike shares, you're in control. You can touch and see the property by inspecting it personally yourself. You can hire a property manager to take the hassles out and manage it for you, for a small tax-deductible fee. You have residual income (rent) coming in year after year, even when you're on holidays. When the property increases in value, all the capital growth and equity are yours to keep. You can get the property manager to inspect it for you and send you pictures.

Investor's tip:

There are four main reasons for investing in property: for capital growth, as collateral to acquire more properties, for rental income to service the debt and to provide positive cash flow income to live off.

Chapter 2.
Property investing for beginner's investors.

Property investing has changed my life and it can change yours too, if you follow the principles in this book. **You can get started in property investing even if you are on a low income by:**

A- Establish a 6 months saving pattern and then apply for a home loan and rent the property out as a shared accommodation.

The tenants (room-mates) will help you pay off the home loan and increase the equity and rental income in the property that you can use to buy another property. A 3-4 bedroom house rented for $100-$150 each room per week, could bring an extra $600-$1,200 in your pocket each fortnight. You can live with your parent for now, while you rent your property. This strategy will benefit you in two ways: providing rental income and tax deductions.

B- Rent the property to overseas students.

Rent the place to 3-4 overseas students. Get some second-hand furniture, and rent it out to them for example, $100-$150 per week. This way you can get $500+ per week. New overseas students are eager to rent this way because it can be hard for them to rent a house on their own. They can't afford the bond and don't have any references. I know of overseas students who are sharing and rented houses privately and paying $120-$150 a week per room each to the landlord. Most students will rent as shared accommodation until they have enough saving and references to move out on their own, or into other accommodation arrangements. Establish proper insurance such as building, content and landlord protection insurance.

C- Get your employer (government) to set aside 20% of your income each pay day.

By the end of the financial year you will have extra fund to invest in a property. It may be difficult to save money yourself.

D- Enter the property with a family member.

You can almost easily buy a home with a family member. Make the property a shared accommodation.

E- Set up a 6-12 months strict budget.

Save all you can for the deposit and establish a saving history.

F- If you have an investment already-use the tax returns funds.

Use this for a deposit on another property.

Why the poor can and should invest too?

Many people fail to understand the importance of investing. You won't know how successful you can be until you try. There are people out of there who are just happy to go to school, leave school as soon as possible, get a job, work hard, buy a flash car and rent a house for the rest of their life. Some will have two to three credit cards and live from pay check to pay check. They will have surplus cash that they will happily spend on consumer goods and going on holidays. Some will eventually get a mortgage and just be happy to work hard and pay it off. They are content with their existence, and will rely on their superannuation and the government to take care of them in old age.

In reality, most of the population and workers in the western world today live like this. They have no long-term goal, and have no plan for retiring early and having financial freedom early in life. They don't think about it, and there are others who think that it is too hard. They view investment as being just for the rich. But if they need money for personal expenses, they are happy to borrow it from the bank. They will not borrow large sums of money to invest. I had this mentality before of following the crowd and not thinking outside the square. I've changed that thinking and mentality now. I view investing as a necessity in today's world.

How to be financially free and retire wealthy quickly?

Returns from property over time come in the form of:

- Capital growth.
- Rental income.

You should buy a property that will give you maximum rental income,costing you very little from your pocket to maintain. The capital growth achieved quickly, will enable you to buy more properties. Remember if you pay too much it will take you a long time to make serious money on the property. **You will have help in your journey to financial freedom by:**

1. Using your tax to cover the shortfall:

After you've decided on the maximum purchase cost you are willing to spend, the next thing is to work out if there's going to be any short-term short-fall or will the property make money from day one.

2. Buying below market value:

To do this you need to know the value of the property first and how much the property has grown since it was built. This will give you an idea of the potential growth prospect of the property. It's important to bargain hard. The longer the property has been on the market, the greater the prospect of getting a better deal.

3. Build your properties rather than buying:

Firstly, you need to find out the value of similar homes in the area. Also, the maximum, medium and average property sales/prices. Find out how much it will cost to build a similar house. This will help you to work out if it will be cheaper to build than buying an established home. It will certainly be cheaper to build than buying. Bargain with the builder and land agents for a couple of thousands dollars discount. This will add to and increase your equity in the property when completed. You should buy/build your first property at a discount to give you instant equity.

You can get started into property investment with very little or no money from your pocket. You only need a full-time job. It is best to consolidate all your personal loans, credit cards and car loan into one big personal loan and borrow extra for the deposit like I did. When the house is completed or increased in value, you can refinance the personal loan into the house.

Property investment expectations: make money.

Since your aim in real estate is to make money, you have to rule out buying property just to pay less tax. Remember to invest you don’t need a lot of of cash from your pocket. You can borrow the equity from your house if you have one to pay for upfront costs. If you don't have a house, you can borrow as a personal loan and use the fund as a deposit with the same bank or with a different institution. Most banks will not ask you where you get the deposit. This is how I got my first property. Soon after, I used this property to acquire three more properties, all within three years.

bigger house and is eager to move on. If so, then there is a greater chance of getting a good deal.

How to make real estate profitable for you.

- Claiming all tax deductions and expenses.
- Using a six months lease and reviewing rent every six months.
- Buy during a slump/slowdown, refinance and reinvest the profits by buying/building more properties.
- Renovations to add value and maximise capital gains.
- Buying capital growth property with good rental income.

Renovation:

Buy the cheapest property in the best street, but below market value. Then renovate the property which will surely increase it's value. Sometimes all that's needed is a little TLC such as new carpet, painting, a new kitchen and landscaping improvements. You need to avoid extensive renovations. This can be costly and blow out your budget. It will destroy the extra equity that you are trying to achieve.

Adding value can be beneficial in two ways:

- Capital gains or increase in property value which can be

used as a deposit for another property.
- Increased cash flow from charging higher rents, as a renovated property will attract tenants prepared to pay more for it.

Table 1- before renovation:

Current value ($430,000) in 2008.
Mortgage-$285,000. Deposit: $15,000. Establishment cost: $20,000
Total property establishment costs: $320,000
Gross capital gain: $110,000.

You've bought the property for $300,000 in 2005, and spent $20,000 on establishment costs. Renovate the property and then revalue it to invest in another property. You need to increase rent.

Table 2- an example of capital gain after property improvement:

Re-valued after renovation: $500,000
Gross capital gain after renovation: $70,000
Renovation cost: $20,000
Net capital gain after renovation: $50,000.

The property has increased in value after renovation by about $50,000. That's an extra equity of $50,000 that you can borrow for another property investment.

Investor's tip:
Think of property investing as the best form of investment and fastest way out of poverty.

What is leverage and why it is the key to wealth creation?
Leverage means borrowing large sums of money using a small deposit on a property or properties as security or sometimes just using the asset to be purchased as security (borrowing at 100%). This means you put down a small outlay and borrow a larger amount of money to invest in appreciated assets. The assets bought should be worth more than the loan. For example, you put down 5% deposit equity in your property and borrow 95% of the purchase costs of the property or properties. You can put down $50,000 or just your house as security and borrow $900,000 to buy or build three properties. These properties should be worth 10%-20% more than what you paid for as you will buy or build below market value. If you do that every two years, in ten years time, you would have made over $2.5 million+ of equity, plus thousands of dollars worth of rental income. By investing $100,000 initially or by using the equity in your house, you have made over $2.5 million in equities in ten years. Combine this with the increasing rental income which will help to service the debt, you can retire from your job.

Investor's tip:

There are four main reasons for investing in property: for capital growth, as collateral to acquire more properties, for rental income to service the debt and to provide positive cash flow income to live off.

Chapter 3.
The benefits of being a property investor.

It is important that you invest wisely in capital growth assets as soon as possible. You need to understand that time is limited. To become financially wealthy, you need to manage your hard earned cash, and not let your lifestyle control you. I quickly realised that I have to control my personal spending habits. You should try and save 10% or more of your income just for investment. If you haven't started to invest, now is the time.
I believe that 6-8 investments and one PPOR (home) fully paid are sufficient for a couple and family to retire comfortably. Anything above this can be too risky for most people. In property investment, it is important to invest safely. Do not let greed get to your head. Be prepared to sell one property, step back and rearrange your finances and go back to the market later if you realised that you've made a mistake. I've experienced this myself in 2007, when I had to sell one of my investments to rearrange my financial position.
With a portfolio of 6 investment property giving you say $1,200 per week cash in hand after expenses, that's $800 a week cash flow after tax income to live off. Rental income will increase each year as rent rises in line with inflation and economic growth. Capital

growth and equity will increase too. Now you have both rising rental income and increasing capital growth on each property annually. Multiply your 6 properties by $5,000-$10,000, that's $30,000-80,000 per year on capital growth alone, money that you can borrow to live off. You can borrow for example, $40,000 each year using an ABN or equity release to top up your income, especially if your total equity position of your portfolio is above 20%. You will not have to declare any income using your ABN or pay lender's mortgage insurance.
The rental income can be used to demonstrate serviceability when applying for a top up on your line of credits. The bank will lend you money on the strength (capital growth and rental income) of your properties alone. It is a wise move to borrow as much money as possible in a line of credit initially, so that you don't have to go back to the bank each year. You can use the money as you desire.
Property investing has opened a whole new window of financial opportunities. There are a lot of people living this way today.
You will be better off investing in property. If you work in the mines or own a business and earn a good income, the tax office will take about half of that income. You have to work very hard, but also smart, otherwise you will be wasting your time. The fact is that the tax system and bank's money can be used to your advantage, if you know how to do it. **The key is to use**:

- Your tax money to set you up to take advantage of the next property boom.
- Bank's money to buy or build more properties, and create wealth to enable you to retire early.

- Your home (PPOR) as collateral to acquire investment properties to further reduce your tax bill, and build wealth in the process.

Importance of saving money to invest in property:

Investing is a forced saving as you are putting money that would otherwise go into consumption of consumer goods into a growth asset; it's a sacrifice. You will get better returns say, in 5-10 years by investing into a $300,000 property than you would do investing anywhere else. Invest wisely in an affordable property in a good location. It is important to note the possibilities and opportunities in borrowing more money to buy more properties as long you can service the loans. Use your home or existing investments to expand your property portfolio.

Let's explore this possibility:

Let's say you have $30,000 (your saving or borrowed money) and you invest $25,000 (keep $5,000 as a buffer) by buying an investment property costing $300,000 but valued at $340,000. You have to fork out $15,000 as a deposit and borrow say $285,000 ($15,000 plus $285,000, 95% LVR) and $10,000 for other establishment costs which are all tax deductible. That's an instant $40,000 in equity. You should always buy a property below its market value. Conduct a property valuation on it before you buy. Use the result of the valuation to bargain with the seller.

Better still, I believe, you will make more instant equity if you borrow money to build a house. If the property increases in value by $10,000 per year. In five years time, the property will be worth at least $390,000. That's a gain of $50,000 in capital growth in five years. If you have 3 such properties, that's $150,000 in equity in five years. How long it will take you to save $150,000? Make sure that you're receiving decent rental income, for example, $300+ per week, and that you've fixed your interest only repayment at a good rate, for example, between 5-7% fixed for 3-5 years. If you are an average worker earning about $60,000 per year, then that's serious money. You will be making more money (equities) than in your day job.

Additionally, considering that you are using your tax and tenants to help you, you're only paying about 25% of the cost of the mortgage, and the tenants and your tax pay the 75% of the cost initially. Essentially, you are paying less $100 per week from your pocket to buy a growth asset which has very little investment risk. Each year your rental income will increase and your contribution to the cost of the property will decrease. Even if you are not making any rental profits yet, you will be benefiting on the capital growth aspect from the investment.

It is important that you invest wisely in capital growth assets as soon as possible. You need to understand that time is limited. To become financially wealthy, you need to manage your hard earned cash, and not let your lifestyle control you. I quickly realised that I have to control my personal spending habits. You should try and save 10% or more of your income just for investment. If you haven't started to invest, now is the time.

I believe that 6 property investment and 1 PPOR (home) fully paid are sufficient for a couple and family to retire comfortably. Anything above this can be too risky for most people. In property

investment, it is important to invest safely. Don't be greedy. Be prepared to sell one property, step back and rearrange your finances and go back to the market later if you realised that you've made a mistake. I've experienced this myself in 2007, when I had to sell one of my investments to rearrange my financial position.
You will be better off investing in property. If you work in the mines or own a business and earn a good income, the tax office will take about half of that income. You have to work very hard, but also smart, otherwise you will be wasting your time. The fact is that the tax system and bank's money can be used to your advantage, if you know how to do it. **The key is to use**:

- Your tax money to set you up to take advantage of the next property boom.
- Bank's money to buy or build more properties, and create wealth to enable you to retire early.
- Your home (PPOR) as collateral to acquire investment properties to further reduce your tax bill, and build wealth in the process.

Importance of saving money to invest in property:
Investing is a forced saving as you are putting money that would otherwise go into consumption of consumer goods into a growth asset; it's a sacrifice. You will get better returns in 5-10 years by investing into a $300,000 property than you would do investing anywhere else. Invest wisely in an affordable property in a good location. It is important to note the possibilities and opportunities in borrowing more money to buy more properties as long you can service the loans. Use your home or existing investments to expand

your property portfolio.

Many people fail to understand the importance of investing. You won't know how successful you can be until you try. There are people out of there who are just happy to go to school, leave school as soon as possible, get a job, work hard, buy a flash car and rent a house for the rest of their life. Some will have two to three credit cards and live from pay check to pay check. They will have surplus cash that they will happily spend on consumer goods and going on holidays. Some will eventually get a mortgage and just be happy to work hard and pay it off. They are content with their existence, and will rely on their superannuation and the government to take care of them in old age.

In reality, most of the population and workers in the western world today live like this. They have no long-term goal, and have no plan for retiring early and having financial freedom early in life. They don't think about it, and there are others who think that it is too hard. They view investment as being just for the rich. But if they need money for personal expenses, they are happy to borrow it from the bank. They will not borrow large sums of money to invest. I had this mentality before of following the crowd and not thinking outside the square. I've changed that thinking and mentality now. I view investing as a necessity in today's world.

Investor's tip:

There are four main reasons for investing in property: for capital growth, as collateral to acquire more properties, for rental income to service the debt and to provide positive cash

flow income to live off.

Now let's look at a situation between an investor and a non-investor.

Investors:	**Non-investors:**
Capital growth.	No wealth.
Rising rental income: returns.	No extra income apart from job.
Good debts on appreciated assets.	Bad debts: cars, credit cards and consumer goods.
Work smarter.	Work harder.
Work less hours with time.	Always and increasingly working harder to meet rising costs of living and paying off bad debts.
-Increasing equities. -More tax deductions for losses and for reducing taxes on positive cash flow.	-Increasing debts. -Little tax deductions. -Increase taxes with increasing income.
Sacrificing now.	Lifestyle- buy now and pay later.
-Will retire early. -More disposable income as they age.	Will retire later in life.
Borrowing equities to invest in appreciating assets.	Borrowing to buy depreciating consumer items.

Live off increasing equities from properties and increasing rental income.	-Live off income from job. -Less disposable income as they age.
Dream and think of ways to invest.	Procrastinating and have little savings and no investment.
-Pay less tax-use taxes to help with the costs of paying for appreciating assets. -Tax minimisation and claiming all legal taxes. -Will retire on a high residual income.	-Pay more tax. -Work beyond normal retirement age. -Retirement income decreases upon retirement.

Investor's tip:

Accumulate more properties (up to 6) as long you can service the loan. Increase the rent each year to provide for cash flow while your interest rates remain fixed.

Successful Real Estate & Property Investment For New investors: how to achieve financial freedom. Revised Edition.

Diagram 1- My investment property in Western Australia:

Part 2-
Understanding property investment.

Chapter 1.
Crunching the numbers before you invest and the importance of investing in cheaper (affordable) but quality property in good locations?

Returns in property come in many ways:

- Good rental income.
- Good capital growth.
- Claiming all tax deductions.

Don't expect your tax saving to cover all the property losses. The rental income must exceed the cost of maintaining the property for this to happen. Two things you need to do before you invest, if you want to be a property millionaire:

- Calculate the potential profits or short term losses from the investments.
- Check the rental growth potential of the property. This will determine affordability.

It is important to buy an affordable property and to keep your losses to a minimum. Keep in mind your capacity to pay. If you are going to buy a larger or more expensive property, chances are that interest rates and maintenance costs would be higher too. This can increase your holding cost and your property losses. It is important to remember that your aim is to accumulate more properties. So, a cheaper negatively geared property can mean that it can become positively geared faster when interest rates fall and rent increases.

Affordability:

The more expensive the property, the greater will be the establishment costs and annual cost to maintain that property. Successful property investors must keep their entry cost down, otherwise the annual maintenance cost is likely to be as high as the entry cost. Affordability is very important and sometimes more important than expected growth. At the end of the day, you will need cash from your pocket to cover the expenses as capital growth cannot be used to pay off the shortfall. Doing this will be self-defeating as you will be destroying (withdrawing) the very equity that you are trying to accumulate. Your debt repayments will also likely to sky-rocket.

Calculating rental returns:

Use the rent (or expected rental return) X by 52 weeks to get the income for the year. Divide the yearly income (sum) by the purchase price. This will give the rental return. Multiply this result by 100 to get the percentage return. For example, a $300 a week rent on a $300,000 property will be as follows: $300 X 52= $15,600. Then divide this $15,600 by $300,000=0.05 rental return. Multiply (X) this by 100 = 5.2 % to get the percentage return.

To calculate rental growth:

You need to calculate and factor in possible increase in property expenses, such as shire rates, interest rates rises, insurance and rate of inflation. You must increase rent accordingly for the investment to be profitable.

Calculating how much the property will cost you before you start investing is a must. Use a spreadsheet or word program.

It is easy to calculate the annual cost of the property before you buy:

1. Calculate interest repayment by multiplying the monthly amount by 12. If interest rates is 6.5% and loan amount is $300,000, we calculate this by: 6.5 X 300= .
2. You need to fix or plan to fix your interest rates as soon as possible for 3 years at a level your comfortable with.
3. Other property expenses such as: shire and water rates, property management fees, insurance and maintenance should cost you about $5,000 per year on a $300,000 property.
4. Add all these property expenses and deduct this sum from the rental or expected rental income. If the result is negative, then you will need to contribute from your pocket to cover the shortfall.

Investor's tip:

Any property losing more than $5,000 before tax can be a problem if you haven't fixed your interest rates. Property losing less than $5,000 per year can be considered as a sound investment but you need to fix your interest rates while you increase rent. Tax deductions will reduce your losses. Ensure that capital growth is promising too.

Below is an example how an investor calculates how much the property will cost him each year and the profitability of the investment before taking the plunge. It shows the importance of crunching the numbers before you buy rather than just buying a property because you can afford it, you can get tax deductions to cover the temporary shortfall, capital gross is promising, or the property seminar presenters say that it is a good investment.

The investor is deciding which one of the three properties (each is a 4 bedrooms and 2 bathrooms) to buy.

Property A and B cost $290,000 and is located in different locations. Property A is in an isolated mining town with a small population of mainly miners and is receiving good rental income but has very little capital growth. Property B is on the out-skirt of the city, in a working class neighbourhood but has greater capital growth of at least 5%+ annually or about $15,000+, consistently for the last 10 years. Property C is in a good area with great capital growth but property prices is higher, $500,000. Interest rate is set at 6.0%. The investor earns $90,000 per year and is taxed at a rate of 30%. Tax paid is $27,000.

Table 1- crunching the numbers before buying:

Property A:	Property B:	Property C:
Rental income: $800 per week or $38,400 per year	Rental income: $500 per week or $24,000 per year	Rental income: $600 per week or $28,800
Interest repayment: $1,740 per month or $20,880 per year	Interest repayment: $1,740 or $20,880 per year	Interest repayment: $3,000 or $36,000 per year
Other expenses: $8,000	Other expenses: $5,000	Other expenses: $10,000
Depreciation deductions: $5,500	Depreciation deductions: $5,500	Depreciation deductions: $7,500
Total property expenses: $34,300	Total property expenses: $31,380	Total property expenses: $53,500
Net rental profit before tax: $4,100+	Net rental loss before tax: $7,380	Net rental loss before

	loss	tax: $24,700 loss.
Taxable income: $94,700	Taxable income: $82,620	Taxable income: $65,300
Tax payable on profits: @$1,000	Tax saving: @$3,000+	Tax saving: @$10,000+

Because the investor has made the effort and crunched the numbers before decided which property to buy, this will help him make the best decision and avoid costly mistakes.

To sum up:

Property A: is making a profit of about $4,100 before tax and around $3,000 after tax but there is little or no capital growth.

Property B: is making a loss of about $7,380 before tax or around $4,500 after tax but there is good capital growth of over $15,000 per year.

Property C: is making a loss of about $25,000 before tax or around $15,000 after tax but there is good capital growth of about 10% or $50,000 per year. Although, this property appears to be the best, but it is expensive. Can you afford it if something such as a recession occurs?

The questions an investor will ask himself before investing:

- Can I afford to cover this loss from your pocket each year until rent increases above property cost?
- Will capital growth increase more than this loss each year to make the investment profitable?

- o Would it be worth it to buy the property in a isolated mining town with very little prospect of capital growth and only about $3,000 of profits per year?
- o Do I invest for capital growth or for rental income or both? It can be hard to find a property with good rental income and good capital growth at the same time.

Affordability is the deciding factor for me as I want to sleep well at night, being able to put food on the table and still able to afford the loan repayment if the property was to be vacant for a couple of months.

Why is it important to buy/build cheaper but quality property in good locations than more expensive ones?

You invest in property for two main reasons:

1. Rental income to make you rich. You can live off the surplus rents.

2. Capital growth to make you wealthy. You can live off the equity.

From my short experience in property investing, I found that the cheaper or more affordable the property, the better. Affordability is the most important aspect of property investing, for without this, you will not be able to achieve the wealth and riches that property investment offers. There is no point in having a large portfolio of 10 or more negatively geared properties that are costing you about $10,000 a year each after tax to keep. That's over $100,000 from your pocket to cover the expenses. Losing too much money in the hope of gaining and offset these losses in capital growth is not a wise idea. It will put too much pressure on your finances, your life and relationship. Property investing is about safe and stress-free investment.

Keep in mind your capacity to pay. If you are going to buy a larger or more expensive property, chances are that interest rates and maintenance costs would be higher too. This means it is better to buy or build 5 X $300,000 investment properties than to buy or build 3 X $500,000 properties. Expensive property can get you into serious financial difficulty if your circumstance changes.

It is important to remember that your aim is to accumulate more properties. So, a cheaper negatively geared property can mean that it can become positively geared faster when interest rates fall or rent increases or both. Also, if you decide to sell your investment property, a $300,000 property is more affordable to most people than a $500,000 property. Any property above $500,000 will attract about 10-20% of buyers compare to say, about 90% of buyers who will be able to afford a $300,00 property. Only about 10-20% of the workforce in the western world is on a very high income. I mean $100,000 or more. Normally, lower end property don't lose their value in a depressed market as much as a higher end or expensive property. Also, there will be less people able and willing to pay high rents on an expensive property. It is easier to rent a $300,000 property at $300 per week than a $500,000 property at $500-$600+ per week.

Why is taking affordability into consideration and crunching the numbers important before you invest?

The more expensive the property, the greater will be the establishment costs and annual maintenance cost to keep that property. Successful property investors must keep their entry costs down, otherwise the annual maintenance costs are more likely to be as high as the entry costs. Crunching the numbers before you buy will ensure that the property is a good investment. You will make money or lose very little money in the short-term. It's not that expensive properties are not good investments, but you would have to have dig deeper into your pocket to maintain such property, unless you can get very good rents, which is very unlikely.

What about maintenance cost and return on the investment?

If you can afford your expensive apartment as a rental, then by all means go for it. Affordability is very important and sometimes more important than expected growth. At the end of the day, you will need cash from your pocket to cover the expenses as capital growth cannot be used to pay off the shortfall. Doing this will be self-defeating as you will be destroying (withdrawing) the very equity that you are trying to accumulate. Your debt and loan repayments will also likely to sky-rocket.

Investor's tip:

It is important to note that all costs associated with buying the property are tax deductible. Most over five years and others when you sell the asset. But you will only get back part of this expense.

Let's see my two property investments as an example of affordable property.
Situation 1- The Vines, in 2009, the cost structure looks like this:
Total annual cost structure:

- Mortgage repayment is $1,400 per month, or $16,800 per year. Shire-rates of $1,200 per year. Water rates and use of about $800.
- Landlord, content, building, public liability insurance of about $800 per year. Property management fees of about $1,500 per year.
- Tax deduction based on my tax rate of 25%. This means that your tax saving will be about 25% of your property losses. My taxable income will be reduced by the losses and I will pay tax on the lower amount.

Total expenses: $21,100.
Gross rental income of $310 per week, or $16,120 per year or about $14,950 net rental income.
Net rental loss before tax or my contribution before tax refund: $16,120-$21,100 = $5,020 or about $100 per week. This property loss is less than $3,000 per year and capital growth is exceeding this loss. Add depreciation benefits of $5,000.
Net property losses: $10,020.
Income of $75,000 and a tax rate of 25%. Tax paid: $18,750.
Tax saving is: 0.25 X $10,020 = @$2,500.
That's a shortfall of about $2,500 or $180 per month or $45 per week. The property is increasing on average of about $5,000-

10,000 per year. I'm about $5,000-$7,000 better off each year.

Situation 2- Let's have a look at my Caversham property:

Rent on the property has increased from $260 to $310 per week in three years. The cheaper the property, the easier and faster it is to achieve cash flow positive.

Total annual cost structure:

- Mortgage repayment is $1,450 per month, or $17,400 per year.
- Shire-rates of $1,200 per year. Water rates and use of about $800.
- Landlord, content, building, public liability insurance of about $800 per year.
- Property management fees of about $1,500 per year.

Total expenses: $21,700.

Rental income of $310 per week = $16,120.

Net rental loss before tax or my contribution before tax refund:

$16,120-$21,700 = $5,580 or $107 per week.

Add depreciation benefits of $5,000.

Property losses: $10,580.

Income of $75,000 and a tax rate of 25%. Tax paid: $18,750

Total net property losses: $20,600. Taxable income: @$54,400.

Tax saving is: 0.25 X $10,500= @$2,500.

That's a shortfall of about $3,000-$3,500 or $300 per month or $65 per week. The property is

Summary:

To sum up, I will say that it is wise to stay away from expensive

investment for the following reasons:

- High mortgage repayments which can mean a longer waiting period to see real capital growth, especially if you've bought during a boom.
- It is harder to refinance expensive property in a depressed market. The property values for expensive property fall much faster than cheaper properties.
- It will take longer for the property to become cash flow positive.
- A 10% to 20% fall in value of a $900,000 property can mean that the property has lost between $180,000-$360,000 of its value compared to a $300,000 property where such a fall in value mean that the property has only lost between $30,000-$60,000 of its value.
- It is easier to sell one of your three $300,000 properties than a $900,000 property as there will be more people able to afford it, especially during a downturn.
- You will be relying a lot more on rental growth to maintain the property than on capital growth.

Have you ever wonder why many property investors go bankrupt? **These are the possible reasons:**

- Buying a property or properties with the heart and not the mind. Not doing the home-work in terms of where to buy for capital growth and good rental prospects.
- Not choosing the property based to it's location. Location doesn't mean close to the ocean. In reality, I will avoid such property because of the price tag. Good locations can mean

close to the city or town centre and close to infrastructure.

- Not doing an independent valuation to ascertain the true value of the property. Buying investment at the height of the boom and paying too much.
- Not fixing the interest rate if the market is buoyant and interest rates are still in early phase of its upward cycle. Not crunching the numbers before you invest.
- If you sell the property to cut your losses, you might make a big loss as due to it's expensive price tag.

Investor's tip:
The more expensive the property, the harder it will be to maintain it. You will have to be receiving very high rent or rent will have to increase substantially for the investment to be profitable. Rising interest rates will multiply your property losses unless you're on a fixed rate.

Chapter 2.

How to build/buy and pay off your family and pay it off within 7-10 years.

If you want to be a successful investor, you will need to understand the lending process and how to apply for a loan. Buying or building your first home is a simple process. You will need to know what house you want and the price range. You should know your borrowing capacity or get a loan pre-approval before-hand. This can easily be done by using the bank's online calculators, or calling a broker and asking him/her about your borrowing capacity or applying for a loan pre-approval. Also, find out before-hand the price of established houses in the area you're thinking of buying. This will ensure that you don't pay too much. It is important that you don't borrow to your limit and that you leave room for your first investment. For example, if your borrowing capacity is $600,000, do not borrow all the $600,000 to build or buy your first home. You should build a house for around $350,000. This will mean that there will be still $250,000 you can borrow to build or buy your first investment. You should avoid building or buying your dream home at first. Focus on acquiring as many property investments in the shortest possible time frame.

Land acquisition and land transfer process:

Carefully select your land and place a $1,000 deposit to secure it while you wait for unconditional finance approval. The land transfer to your name will take about two months.

The building contract and building process:

The land agent will be able to give you a list of builders. You can call these builders and ask them for the price range of the house you have in mind. Ask them to send you some brochures, with prices included. Some builders have their own broker. Your builder will ask for a $1,000 to draw your house plan. Ensure that the builder fix the construction cost for 45 days while you wait for finance approval.

Make sure that you like the design and the price of the building before you sign off the plan. When it comes to signing the contract for the building, it is important that you agreed on a price, written and sign by both parties. The builder will supply you with a cost schedule and building contract approved by council. Upon receiving the signed contract, the house plan and cost schedule from you, the builder will sign and forward back to you two copies of these documents. One set of documents that you will supply to the bank before the unconditional finance approval, and the other for your record. When finance is formally approved, the construction of your house can begin. The loan application will take about three weeks. You will need to inform the builder when finance is formally approved.

It will take about 3-6 months for the paperwork to be completed and about 6-12 months for the house to be completed. Once, you've received the keys to your new property, you can complete the landscaping and paving. Normally most land agents will provide fencing and front landscaping as part of their package.

The construction process:

- Within six months, the builder will start construction on your house.
- After the first stage of the house is completed, they will send you an invoice to let you know of this. You have ten working days to sign off on each construction stage. Fax the construction loan form to the bank to authorise payment to the builder.

When it comes to the fifth stage, the builder will invite you to inspect the house. If you're satisfied with the house/work, you will be ask to sign off the final stage (finance) of the house. You should fax the final construction/invoice form to the bank. You will then have the keys to your house, usually within three weeks.

Let's sum up the process:

- Check your borrowing capacity online.
- Visit land agents and builders to look for suitable land or land and house package.
- Place a deposit on the land.
- Apply for finance for the land first or for both house and land at the same time.

Pre-start interview:

Before starting construction on your house, the builder will invite you to a pre-start meeting. If you cannot come, they will post you a pre-start book for you to select the interior of the house, such as flooring types, brick selection, door knobs, roof design, colour and so on. You will need to call the gas, electricity and phone companies to set up an account number. At the meeting you need to have:

- Your gas and electricity account number.
- Your cheque book if you are planning to do a bit of upgrading such as flooring.
- A copy of your land title and your completed pre-start book.
- At the builder's office they will have sample of features (door knobs and roof tiles) for you to select.

After you've done your research and ready to buy, this is what you need to do have:

A- A deposit:

Lenders generally require 5-20% deposit of the purchase price.

B- Pay stamp duty:

The more expensive the property, the higher will be the stamp duty payable, as it is a percentage of the purchase price of the property. .

C- Pay settlement agent fees:

This can cost around $1,000. Look for them in the Yellow Pages.

D- Pay bank and lender's mortgage insurance (if applicable) fees:

- **Loan application fees:** $500-$800.
- **Loan valuation fees:** about $300-$1,000 for each property.
- **Other fees:** title searches which will cost around $150.

E- Pest control and building inspections fees.

How to pay off your home(PPOR) sooner?

You can pay off a mortgage within 7-10 years by using a clever financial structuring in conjunction with a property investment. This is more effective when you:

1. Research and negotiate with your lender:

It is important to monitor the market regularly to keep up-to-date with new products. Examine your current loan and compare this to that of other lenders. Ask your lenders for a better deal or if they can match what's on offer in the market.

2. Pay extra on your home:

The fastest way to pay off your home (PPOR) is to make extra repayments and pay fortnightly rather than monthly. Also, you can use an offset account and make monthly loan repayment. Even $100 per fortnight will save thousands and cut years off your home loan (PPOR).

3. Reduce your spending habits:

Make small changes to your spending habit. For example, take lunch to work instead of buying, cancelling the gym membership and working out at home.

4. Reduce credit card debt:

Refinance your credit cards to another bank which has a 0% interest balance transfer for six months.

5. Don't be attracted by low interest loans:

Look at the total cost of borrowing and comparison rates, not just the interest rate. Get a broker to work that out for you. Some low rates are achieved through higher account keeping, redraw, monthly and annual fees.

6. Check your home loan statements:
Human and even computer errors are responsible for mistakes in your home loans costing you thousands. Make sure that you're being charged the right amount and the right interest rate. Buy a software called "Mortgage Watchdog" costing $180 for this purpose. Visit:www.mortgagewatchdog.com for a copy.

Let's see the strategy that I'm using that many savvy investors use too.

A- PPOR (home loan) and offset account are linked together:
The PPOR has an offset account link to it. All rental incomes from the three investments are deposited into this offset account.

B- Offset account:
All mortgage repayments will be deducted from this offset account. So, money in this account will reduce your loan balance and interest bill.

Diagram showing features of an offset account:

-Money available in an instant at ATM. **-No interest paid.** **-No tax paid on this amount.** **-Good for property investors and, especially, for people receiving cash flow positive income but still have debts.**	**-Get no bank interest rate payment on the loan balance.** **-Interest on the home-loan attached to the account is reduced by the amount in the offset account or the loan balance.** **-Money is in your account.**

C- Credit card:

Use the credit card to pay off bills such as rates, electricity and gas, food and petrol, while more money sits in the offset account to reduce the interest bill on your PPOR. Pay off the balance in full before the due date.

D- Line of credit:

Get a line of credit, for example, $100,000 limit. You can withdraw $50,000, and deposit this in the offset account to cover the shortfall on the property investment. You can claim tax deductions on the interest payment on the line of credit as long it is being used for investment purposes. The $50,000 will reduce the interest bill on the PPOR. All loan repayments should come out of your offset account.

Diagram showing features of a line of credit:

-Like a big credit card. -Home loan interest rates. -Interest charge on amount withdrawn. -Interest only payment or principal and interest. -Tax deductible if used for investment purposes.	**-Pre-approved: say, $100,000. -Linked to your mortgage but as a separate account. -Money can be withdrawn online or over the phone by increment of $5,000 each time. You will have the money into your bank/offset account in two-three days. -If more money is needed, then ask for a cheque book linked to this line of credit.**

	-Money is in the bank's account.

Diagram- a monthly financial structure:

MONTHLY FINANCIAL STRUCTURE

PPOR (Cost $300,000)
$67.000
$233,000 Balance
*Interest rate fixed at least 50% and 50% flexible

Investment
Rental Income $1,000/month
Rental Income $1,000/month
Rental Income $1,000/month

Offset Account $67,000

Wages: $4,000/month

Credit Cards: $10,000

Line of credit: $100,000 Balance : $50,000

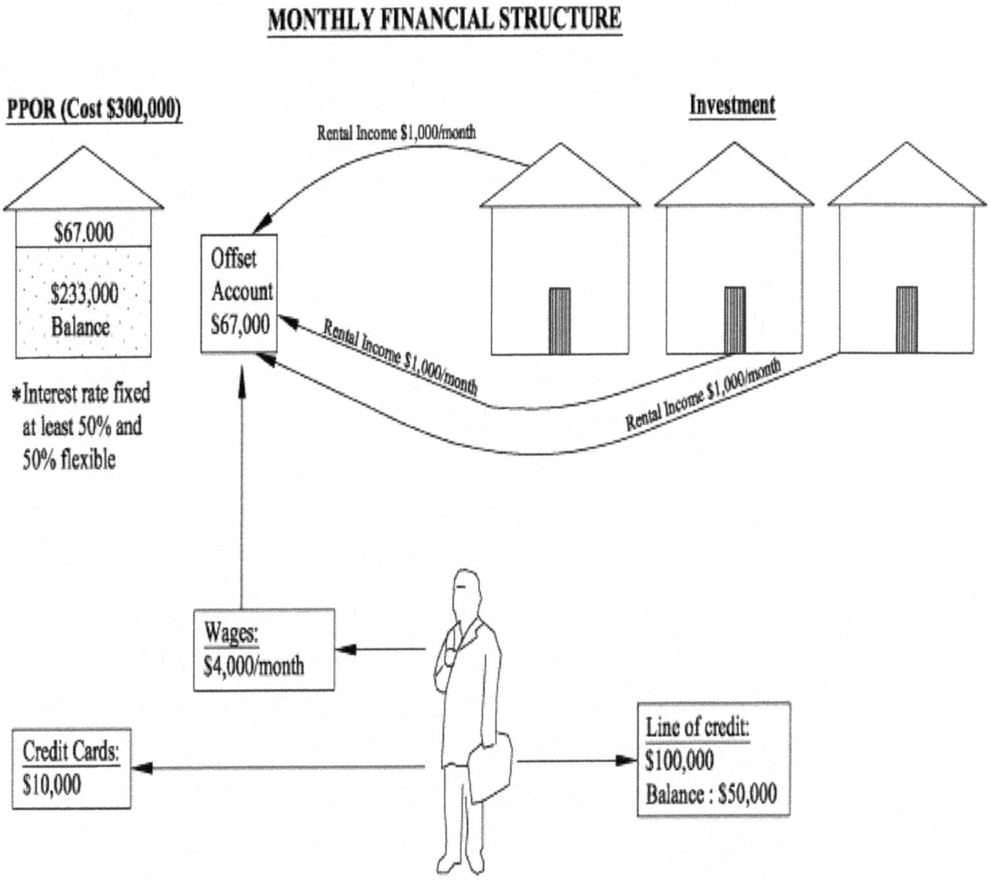

You use a '55 days interest free credit card' to pay off all bills and groceries. Deposit all your incomes (rental income and PAYG) into an offset account to reduce your interest bill daily. Pay off the credit card balance before it is due.

In this way:

- You will be paying less interest on the home loan.
- Paying chunks off the principal on the home loan.
- Making your wages and tax deductions work harder for you.
- You will own your home outright in 10 years instead of 20-30 years.

How to buy/build your first investment property?

A-Equity release to build or buy your first investment property:

After you've built your first home and ready to buy your first investment, you can apply for an equity release in the form of a line of credit. Then apply for an investment loan and use the fund in the line of credit for the deposit. You can apply for the investment loan with the same bank or with a different institution. This way, you will have succeeded in borrowing a 100% for the investment loan.

Investor's tip:

Until the property is completed, the lender will only value the property at whatever the land cost you, plus the building cost. Once the property is completed, you can have it valuated and borrow more money from it. You will not be able to fix the interest on the loan until the house is completed. You cannot totally eliminate the risk involved in property investment, but you can reduce it as much as possible.

Chapter 3-
Why is it important to buy your own house and use it to achieve financial freedom?

It has always been my view that rent money is dead money. The point is that you are paying for someone else's property. Why not buy your own home (PPOR) as soon as you can? You might even buy a house with your sibling as joint owners and then use the extra cash you've saved to invest in an investment property. Only invest with someone else as a last resort.

Let's have a look at what happens when you rent a property rather than buying one?John decides not to buy a house but rent instead.

Table 1- renting a property:

Rent money:	Rent money:	Rent money:	Rent money:	Rent money:
$600 per fortnight.	$1,200 per month.	$14,400 per	$72,000 in five	$144,000 in ten

		year.	years.	years.

In ten years, it would have cost John about $144,000 in rent payments. That is precious money that has helped the landlord pay off his mortgage. John has gained nothing from this transaction.

What happens if John has made some sacrifices and bought a $300,000 property instead?

Table 2- buying a property:

Mortgage payment:	Mortgage payment:	Mortgage payment:	Mortgage payment:	Mortgage payment:
$600 per fortnight.	$1,200 per month.	$14,400 per year.	$72,000 in five years. Equity of at least 25% of the property value.	$144,000 in ten years. Reduce some of the debt. Equity growth of at least 50% of the property value.

The diagram above shows that if you sacrifice a bit and buy your own house, in ten years time you will make at least $150,000 in capital growth on a $300,000 property.

The advantages of buying a property rather than renting are listed below.

So, by buying a property, John would be at least $150,000 better off. He can use the equity to buy 1-2 investment property. This can mean 1-2 X $150,000+ in capital growth within ten years. I will use my situation as an example. I've rented 5 different properties for about 4 years before buying one myself. I hated the hassles of property inspection and constant moving.

Diagram- renting a property compare to buying one in 10 years.

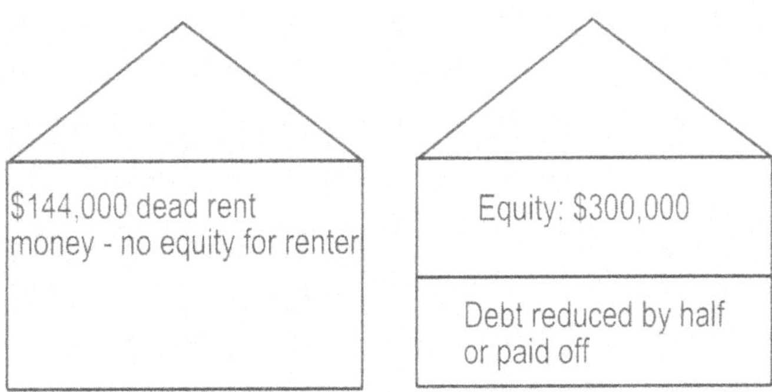

It has been shown that buying a house is more advantageous than renting because:

- You benefit from capital growth of at least $5,000 per year.
- You can use the tenants (rental income) and tax benefits to help pay off your mortgage.
- You can reduce the debt on the house quickly by using an offset account. For example, if you can save $400 per month, in ten years, you would have saved between $50,000-

There are three main reasons for home ownership:

1. Avoid renting someone else's property forever and be at the mercy of the landlord and rent increases:

Rent savings can be used to make mortgage repayment and the property can be yours in the end. You will not have to ask the property manager if you can paint the house or have regular home inspections.

2. As a life-line for urgent personal expenses such as a much needed new car.

You can use the house to finance personal expenses such as a much needed new car or cash to pay bills. Many people hate borrowing money from their house to pay for personal expenses. But I think there are times when you should. It is cheaper to finance a car from your house equity than getting a personal loan or finance through a car dealer.

3. For investment purposes to grow your portfolio and to create wealth.

Educated and well-informed people use their house not as 'a great Australian or American dream,' but as a means to create wealth and achieve financial freedom. The majority of home-owners don't think or see property that way. They see their home as a great dream, but has to be paid off as soon as possible. They have the mentality that investing is too risky and are afraid of losing their family home. You will be better off if you treat your house as an investment engine and a way for creating wealth.

Very few people have lost their home by using it to invest, if they've invested wisely. You can sell one of your investments a few years down the track and pay off your home sooner. The conventional way like most people do, will take you at least 25 years and cost you thousands of dollars in interest.

Why property should be viewed as a wealth creation and not 'as an Australian or American dream?'

By using your home to invest in 2 properties, you will be better off in 10 years. You could sell one of the investment 7-10 years later and use the proceed to pay off the family home. You will need to move into this investment and declaring it as your PPOR while selling it, to avoid capital gains tax. If both partners are working then investing should not be a scary thing. You will not be better off owning only one house.

Why you should avoid directing all excess funds into paying off the PPOR but instead use it for property investment purposes?

It is a fact of life that we've been taught by our parents to avoid getting into debt. Apart from the minority of kids from rich families accustomed to investing and taking risks, most of us have no concept of investing. We only know that we need to work hard to look after ourselves and our family. We get a job and save for a big deposit on a house. Then we direct all our resources into paying it off house. Most people rarely view a house as a springboard to accumulate more investments. Paying off your home gives you no tax deductions and will not create wealth and residual income that you can use to live off later.

You can pay off the house much faster by:

- By buying two or more investment properties.
- You can use your tenants and taxes to help you maintain the properties.
- In ten years time, one of the investments will have grown in value. You can sell it and use the proceeds to pay off the family home (PPOR).
- By using a smart financial structure explained in the book.
- In 10 years time, you can be debt free, and have no mortgage on your PPOR and some investment property.

You need to note that in the first ten years of paying off a home loan, 80% of the payment is for interest payments and not the principal. So, it makes more financial sense to have property investments. Why do I say 10 years, and not 5 or 15 years? Research has shown that it roughly takes about 10 years for a property to double in value. Property investment should be done safely. This means avoiding buying expensive properties and investing in positive cash flow property instead. Every time you have extra equity, borrow money and leave some in a line of credit and withdraw most and deposit it into your offset account. The money in the offset account is better than cash in a saving bank account. You will not pay any tax on the funds in the offset account. Using your equity this way is more advantageous than leaving the equity in your family home untouched. Investing wisely will pay dividends for you in the future.

Chapter 4-
The importance of understanding the property cycle, and the effects of rising interest rates on your property portfolio.

It is important to note that interest repayment is the largest expense that a property owner has to make. It can make or break an investor. So, it is very important to keep interest rates under your radar at all times.

Three important things to note about interest rates:

1. Interest rates are more likely to rise than fall.
2. Your repayment is likely to rise than fall unless you've fixed your interest rates.
3. When your portfolio is doing well (boom), interest will be on the rise too.

With this information in mind, it is wise to assume that interest rates will likely to rise and cause problems for investors and even home-occupiers who are unprepared.

The most important thing to consider before buying an investment property is the expenses and returns. Firstly, you need to consider, the interest rates and loan repayment:

The importance of fixing your loans:

Rising interest rates can be disastrous for novice and unprepared investors. When interest rates rose from 6% in 2006 to about 9% in 2007, repayments went up by 30% on each of my four loans. I was totally caught unaware and struggled to stay afloat. As I placed the Busselton property on the market, high interest rate cut quickly into my equity and profit. This meant that when I finally sold the property at Busselton, I lost about $30,000 in high interest payments. I learnt the hard way of not fixing your interest rate.

Rising interest rates can put a big strain into your property investment funds unless you're careful. When I started in property investment, I didn't realise the importance of understanding interest rate movements. Any changes to interest rate add to your repayments. I have the opportunity to fix my interest rates at about 7% for three years in early 2007, but didn't. When interest started to rise at the end of 2006, I thought it will go up and then down. I didn't realise that it was going up, and up for a while and the impacts that it will have on my repayments. It cost me about $40,000 in 18 months. Have I fixed my rate, even for one year at the start of 2007, it will have save me about $40,000.

The mistake I made at the start of my investment property career was to refinance my property at Mandurah directly by increasing the mortgage from $200,000 to $278,000 instead of borrowing this extra cash as a line of credit of $80,000. It will take me a bit longer to pay off my PPOR. I should have left the PPOR mortgage at $200,000. However, I deposited the $70,000 profits I made on the sale onto the house (PPOR). Have I borrowed the money as a line of credit, I would have reduced the mortgage on the PPOR to $120,000 instead of $256,000 as it is now. That's an excellent strategy: paying off this non-tax-deductible asset of PPOR as soon as possible and claim the interest payment from the investment on my tax. If I've shopped around for a cheaper builder, I could have saved an extra $25,000 on the Busselton property and I would have had $105,000 to put on my PPOR mortgage, reducing it to less than a $100,000, as that was my strategy. My aim was to keep the Busselton for a few years, maybe for seven years until it goes up in value then sell it to pay off my PPOR .

The dangers of rising interest rates:

The dangers of rising interest rates to property portfolio were evident in 2007 in Australia, when mortgage defaults rose sharply, as interest rates reached 9.5%. Rising interest rates can be disastrous for novice investors. My loan repayments went up by 30%. I was caught unprepared. As I placed the Busselton property on the market, high interest rates increased my property losses and reduced my equity and profits. This means that when I finally sold the property at Busselton, I lost about $40,000 in high interest payments.

A 2% interest rates rise on a $300,000 mortgage will mean paying an extra $500 per month and $1,000 on a $600,000 mortgage. When

I started in property investment I didn't realise the importance of understanding interest rate movements. I had the opportunity to fix my interest rates at about 6.5% for three years in 2006, but didn't. I didn't know the impact that rising interest rates will have on my loan repayments. You can fix all or part of your loan if you're worried interest rates may rise in the next few years. This will provide certainty of loan repayments and for rental increases to have its greatest impact of allowing you to buy another property.

Interest rates rises:

Now let's look at a situation when interest rates go up by two percent from 5% to 7%, with a variable interest rate. The investor's properties are cash flow positive. The total debt is $885,000. Other things stay the same but mortgage repayments on his three properties went up.

Situation 1- before interest rates rises

An investor with three positive cash flow properties and interest rates of 5% variable and interest only repayment.

Property 1- mortgage of $200,000. Rent of $320 per week.

Property 1	$200,000
Rental income:	$16,640
Other expenses:	$3,000
Total interest rates repayment @$800 p/week:	@$10,000
Total property expenses:	$13,000

Rental gain:	**$3,640+**
Cash flow positive:	**$3,640.**

His property portfolio is said to be cash flow positive by about $3,640+ before tax.

Situation 2- Interest rates has increased to 7%, with variable and interest only loan.

Table 1- before tax:

Property 1	$200,000
Rental income:	$16,640
Other expenses:	$4,000
Total interest rates repayment @$1,120p/month:	@$13,440
Total property expenses:	$17,440
Rental loss:	**$800 loss.**

His property portfolio has moved from being cash flow positive of about $4,000 before tax to being negatively geared with a loss of about $800 before tax. So, a 2% increase in interest rates has led to about $5,000 increased in property cost/loss before tax. If interest rates were to rise further, say be another 2%, he will be making more after tax losses. This is a situation that should be avoided at all costs, by fixing your interest rates early.

Situation 3- interest rates increased to 9%.

Property 1	$200,000
Rental income:	$16,640
Other expenses:	$3,000
Total interest rates repayment per month:	@16,880
Total property expenses:	$19,880
Rental loss:	**$3,240**

Rising interest rates have increased his property cost by an extra $2,400 before tax. The more expensive the property, the greater will be your repayment increase (contribution) and your after tax losses.

Understanding the property cycle.

It is important to understand the property cycle. If you don't know, ask or research to ensure that you don't pay too much and buy in the right cycle or in a downturn instead of an upswing. **The property market has four stages:**

A- Upswing/boom: rent and property values going up in most places and rapidly in other places.

If you're thinking of buying, ensure that you look for a good deal and avoid paying too much. I believe that the market will stabilise at the end of this year and start to recover in mid 2011 and move into an upswing in early 2012. It will be nice if you've bought in 2008-2010, when the market was depressed. You will now be reaping the benefits of capital growth. This is also a time when interest rates will rise too. Renters will be forced to compete with each other for limited stocks and cheap property. They will be willing to pay higher rents for a good property, especially a new one.

B- Slowdown: property values slowing down and falling in most places.

The property market slows down after a boom. This is the time when the media is talking unfavourably about the property market. Smart investors will take advantage of the sluggish market and buy properties at bargain prices. As long as you can afford the property, it's quality built and in a good location, you should hold on to it. The market will recover. It is the best time to squeeze in another property before the market recovers fully.

C- Downswing/recession: property values reaching its lowest level in decades.

I believe that the best time to buy is when the property market has slowed down totally and property is losing its value. It is a buyer's market. This is a time when interest rates will be falling and property investments will be more affordable. That's why I believe that 2010 is the best time to buy.

D- Recovery: rent and property values starting to increase in

most places after a period of flat or falling property values/prices.

As more people rush in to buy, prices will rise and interest rates will move up too. Rent will rise to keep pace with economic growth. If you buy properties in this period, make sure that you don't overpay. It takes 7-10 years for the property market to complete a full cycle.

Part 3-
Understanding the financial aspect of property investing.

Chapter 1-
It is easy to invest in property.

Before investing you should:

- Check your borrowing capacity online.
- Visit land agents and builders to look for suitable land or land and house packages.
- Place a deposit on the land. Apply for finance for the land first or for both house and land at the same time.

How to understand the money lending process?

Financial institutions look at three factors when assessing your loans:

(a) Loan to valuation ratio (LVR).
(b) Your existing debt versus assets: debt servicing ratio (DSR).
(c) Your existing incomes (rental, PAYG and other incomes).

Loan to valuation ratio (LVR):

This means that they will order a valuation on your property when you apply for a loan to buy another property, for a line of credit or equity release but not for personal loan or credit cards. They will also lend against the strength of the property value (and your equity), and taking into account your income and rents to calculate your serviceability. This will protect the banks against defaults and losing money as they are not lending more than what the property is worth and based on your ability to repay the loans. It is also used by the banks to decide if you need to pay lender's mortgage insurance and how much to pay. If the property value is low, you will not be able to borrow as much money or lender's mortgage insurance will be higher. For example, borrowing $300,000 for a property costing $315,000, will mean a 95% LVR. It will cost you about $8,000 in lender's mortgage insurance. While the same property with a borrowing of 85% LVR, might cost you about $3,000 in lender's mortgage insurance. If you buy a property below its market value, for example, a $400,000 property for $300,000, the LVR is 75% and therefore, no lender's mortgage insurance is payable as you're borrowing below 80% LVR and within the banks' safe lending zone. Generally, it is easier to borrow below 80% LVR than above this.

Debt servicing ratio (DSR):

This works by taking into account all your incomes including rental income minus your total commitment of debt repayments. This will determine if you can afford the loan. They will also consider your other expenses such as credit cards, personal loans and other home loan repayments. The more expenses/commitments you have, the less they will be willing to lend you, unless you're on a very high income and have a lot of properties with a high level of equity in them. Most lenders prefer your debt service ratio (DSR) to be between 30-40% of your PAYG income but will include 75% of rental income in the calculation. You can increase your borrowing capacity by completing a tax variation and consolidating all your personal debt into one loan or refinance your personal debt into your home-loan to reduce loan repayments.

Assets and liability:

They will look at all your debt (investment and non-investment) and personal assets to determine your capacity to repay the debt. Like:

a) How much you are borrowing.
b) The level of deposit your contributing (LVR) or asset you're using as security.
c) If you have enough incomes to service the new debt.
d) Saving history.
e) If you have a clean or good credit and no criminal history.

If you pass these test, they will advance the loan to you.

Let's have a look at refinancing existing loan for equity release or buying another property.

Table 1- assets and debts:

Assets & equities	**Debts:**
-Three properties: total value of assets of $1,200,000. -Current equity: $400,000. -Possible extra borrowing without income declaration using your ABN (business number):	-Total debts: $800,000. -LVR: 66%. -The investor can increase debt to $960,000 or borrow an extra $160,000.

up to $960,000. -Equity is now only 20% or $240,000.	-LVR is now 80%. No lender's mortgage insurance to be paid.

As shown, the investor can increase his debt to $960,000 or borrow an extra $160,000 fairly easily as the LVR is below 80%.

Another example:

Assets:	**Debts:**
Home (PPOR): valued at $430,000	$320,000
Investment property 1: valued at $470,000	$280,000
Bank balance: $25,000	$1,000. Credit card: limit $5,000
Your gross income (monthly): $4,000	
Superannuation: $5,000	
Total assets: $900,000.	**Total debts: $605,000.**

To work out your current LVR and LVR up to 80%

A) Using the above example: the current LVR is: $900,000

divide by 100 X 80% LVR=$720,000. The investor can borrow an extra $115,000 without declaring his income or even if his income is limited as he is borrowing below the bank's safety zone- below 80% LVR.

You can borrow up to $720,000 or an extra $115,000 as property improvements or as a deposit to buy/build a new property. For a buffer loan, you have to borrow the fund as a 'renovation' loan and leftover money can be set aside as a reserve fund.

Refinancing fees that you should be aware of:

Let me educate you on some of the fees that you will be charged when you refinance from one bank to another or refinance with the same bank. When I bought the land at Busselton, I had to contribute some funds towards the purchase. It is hard to get 100% finance in today's world. Lenders expect you to contribute at least 3% of the cost of the asset as security. This contribution can be as much as 20% depending on:

- **The economic environment:** in a recession or financial crisis like in 2008-09 lenders were asking for at least 20% deposit.
- **Your income:** the higher your income, the more lending institutions will be willing to lend you money. But they will still expect a bigger contribution when you borrow more money if this is your first loan.
- **If both partners are working:** if both partners apply as the main applicants or the other as guarantor, the more banks will be willing to lend you.
- **The stability and the length of working history:** if you've

been working and investing for a while and have never default on any loan, the safer you are in the eyes of lenders.

- **The value of the property:** if you are buying below market value or better if it's a bargain.
- **The amount of saving and your saving history:** the greater the amount of saving and the longer your saving history, the more money you can borrow.
- **The cost of the property:** the more expensive the property, the riskier it may look in the eyes of the lender due to the amount of loan repayment you have to make.
- **The amount of your other debt and liabilities:** the more personal loans and credit cards you have, the less money you can borrow due to the higher repayments and because there are no incomes or returns from these loans.
- **Risk:** the cleaner your credit history and job stability, the higher will be your lending valuation ratio (LVR), the greater the amount they will lend you.
- **Discharge fees:** it can cost you thousands in refinancing and discharge fees as well as fees to set up the new loan with the new bank.

Let's summarise the cost of refinancing my loan ($140,000) to Westpac Bank and to get a construction loan. A total loan of $288,000 to give you an idea of what's involved and payable to the new lender alone:

Lender's mortgage insurance:	$4,574
Progressive draw-down fee:	$200
Annual package fee:	$395

Registration charges account: $82
Stamping charges account: $582.

All these fees will come out of your of the amount of money you're borrowing. All these fees are tax deductible and claimable over 5 years.

After doing your research and you're ready to invest, this is what you need to pay:

A- A deposit:

Lenders generally require a 5-20% deposit of the purchase price. For example, for
a $300,000 mortgage, you will need between $15,000 and $30,000. Some banks in good times will ask for a 3% deposit, which means only $9,000 on a $300,000 loan. In bad times, banks will ask between 10-20% deposit. In this current market, I will buy a property investment for around $300,000- $350,000.

B- Stamp duty:

You also need to pay stamp duty. The more expensive the property, the more the stamp duty will be, as it is a percentage of the purchase price of the property. On a $300,000 loan, you will need around $10,000 in stamp duty for an investment property, and lower for first home buyers. Other states and countries have different costs structures and these fees can change due to government policies. So, check this out and factor this cost into your purchase.

C- Settlement agent fees:

This can cost around $1,000. Settlement agents will smooth out the purchase transactions for you. Shop around and you'll get a good discount. All my settlement agent fees cost around $800. Look for them in the Yellow Pages.

D- Bank fees:

You will need to pay LMI (lender mortgage insurance) which only protects the lender in case you default on the loan, if you borrow more that 80% of the purchase price. This can be around 2.5% of the loan amount. For example, a $300,000 loan in which you borrow 90% of the loan, will end up costing you $5,000-$10,000 in lender's mortgage insurance. LMI can be deducted from the loan amount or capitalised into the loan.

- **Loan application fees:** about $500-$800. Some banks will waive this fee.
- **Loan valuation fees:** about $300 for each property. Sometimes the banks absorb the costs of this.
- **Other fees:** such as title searches which will cost around $150.
- Generally, you need to set aside about $10,000 for all these costs.

E- Pest control and building inspections fees:

It is wise to have a termite and building inspections before you buy a property. This will cost you around $500 for both.

Pre-approval of your loan:

When your deposit is ready, you will need to get a loan pre-approval from the bank. This will involve you applying for a loan for the purchase price of property if you're buying or a pre-approved amount. Then go shopping with the pre-approval letter which will usually last for three months.

What do you need to get your first home loan approved?

- Two of the last or most recent pay slips.
- Last tax return if you have one.
- Identification: driver's license and bank cards.
- Bank statements showing personal loan or credit card repayments.

To get your first investment you will need:

1. Two of the last or most recent pay slips.
2. Last tax return.
3. Identification: driver's licence and bank cards
4. Council and water rates.
6. Bank statements showing mortgage repayments.

I made the decision four years ago to try property investment for my early retirement. It is easy to invest in property once you've bought your first home or first investment. Many home-buyers don't know how much they can afford to borrow and other basic lending details until they apply for a loan. It pays to be informed in today's world. If you can manage regular rent repayment, then it is possible that you can afford an average home ($300,000) that cost four times your gross (income before tax) annual income. Sometimes, you just have to add a $100 a week on top of the rent you're currently paying and you're off to home ownership. It is better to pay extra money and buy your own house rather than help paying for someone else's house.

You can duplicate that by using the equity later on to buy an investment property costing you very little or nothing, when you claim all taxable deductions. Rather having no home, you'll soon have two or three properties. The best part about property is that you can go to the bank and borrow money on it for all sort or purposes.

The key to a good home loan is to save for a deposit of at least 20% to avoid lender's mortgage insurance. Many institutions require only 5-10% deposit. Most lenders require a regular saving history but remember, I didn't have a good saving history and yet I was approved a loan. It was hard to save money and I was spending more than my income through my credit card. Property investing forced me to save. The key to home ownership is to have a job for more than 6 months that pays a decent wage rather than having a good saving record. Not many people can save for a 20% deposit. The bank will lend you based on your other financial commitments, your income and job stability rather than your deposit. It is important to have a cash reserve of three months to cover unexpected expenses. So, don't use all your deposit but keep some as a 'buffer' for a few months of repayment and borrow the rest from your lender.

Ask your lender to explain all the fees, including stamp duty, loan establishment costs, mortgage insurance if required and any other upfront costs. Most lenders will lend about 30-40% of your total income on your home (PPOR). For example, if your income is $1,200 a fortnight, your mortgage repayment should be about $500 a fortnight. But remember it is easier to borrow the equity from your house for an investment property as 75% of rental income is taken into account for calculating your mortgage serviceability by the banks.

Better still you can give yourself another advantage by claiming your tax deductions now and increase your income when you approach the bank for an investment loan. So, once you've acquired an investment property for at least 6 months, you can borrow the equity to buy another investment property. Quality property lose their value much slowly in a slowdown than other properties.

Almost everyone would like to be wealthy but not many have the courage and knowledge of how to achieve this. When I started investing in property in 2005, I was a bit scared but soon (2006) I was building two properties at the same time. My friends thought that I was crazy. I was determined to let this get to me. I wanted to be able to have the money to go places and buy things for my family and realised that I will be better off borrowing large sums of money rather than not borrowing and investing at all.

Life is too short to be doing the same old things all the time like going to work back and forth, and not being able to show for the hard work. Also, having little in my bank account but crippling credit card debt. This is not the way I wanted to end my working life. After reading a couple of books on property investment and how ordinary Australians are doing well in property, I wanted to be a part of the game.

As I looked back on my journey in property investment, my advice for people thinking of taking the plunge, is to go out there and give it a try. You have to ignore negative people who tell you that it is too risky. I believe that most people can invest safely in property. The key is knowledge and in this book I have outlined in easy steps how I did it.

How can your home be the key to accumulating investment

properties?

- Once you've bought your first home (PPOR) and used the home-buyers grant, the bank will be willing to lend you money for your first investment.
- This is because they can rely on your home as collateral or security for the investment. They also know that people will do everything to protect and service their mortgage. The banks want to get you as a client and buying an investment is added business for them. They want to tap into your existing home equity and know that using your home will provide them with interest payments and profits.
- By using your home and your first investment as securities you can give yourself the edge by borrowing the bank's money to set you off on your quest to financial freedom. It is a matter of buying the right property and wait for the equity and rental income to grow. It is important not to over-commit yourself and allow time to help grow your investment.

Property investment is not a get rich scheme. However, it is not hard to invest in property. You just need the knowledge that you can gain just by buying and reading books and attending free property seminars. To be a good property investor you need to understand interest rates and its effect on your portfolio and ways to protect your position. There is also a section on the debate on cross-securitisation and the benefits and disadvantages of it. I've also included notes on how to structure your loan for ease of accessing equity for property accumulation and the things you should avoid.

You can get started by buying investment and living with your parents.

If you can't buy your first home as PPOR now you can get started by buying an investing property first. You can use your tax and the tenant to pay for the expenses. As your income increases, you can buy another investment. This will maximise your deductions and capital growth; the rental income and your taxes can cover all or most of the losses or shortfall. You can make losses on a quality property but it will be covered by your tax, unless it is a very expensive investment that your taxes cannot cover the losses. Then this property is a mistake. Avoid buying an expensive property. Even if you make some rental losses, this is not a problem unless the property value is not increasing at all. Then you have to sell and buy elsewhere as the equity (fuel for property growth) is not being realised. As you continue to live with your parents or sharing a rented house, you can use any extra cash for investment purposes. You will come up on top in the end this way.

Why not investing is costing money every year?

I was amazed when I got my first tax return of $4,000 and my wife $2,500 in 2006, just because we built our first house and rented it out for one year while we were working away from home. That was amazing, having a house that's growing in value and using our taxes to pay for it, that fantastic. I was earning over $50,000 and paying about $13,000 in taxes. It was costing me over $13,000 a year by not investing.

Buying big and expensive houses for the rental market could be a mistake and costly.

One of the biggest mistake investors make is buying a property that is difficult to rent and achieve maximum (but not excessive) rent. This can mean a large property with surplus bedrooms (5 bedrooms) that tenants are not using and you've paid a premium for it. The average number of persons per household in Western world is 2.5 while many property investments are four bedrooms instead of three bedrooms. Buying bigger homes as investment can be costly and many investors will effectively be wasting up to $100,000 dollar just by buying homes with vacant rooms that will never bring in additional rents. If you're investing in the city, the rental returns can be low compared to the expensive cost of the apartment.

Steps in getting into the property ladder faster and easier.

There is a simple process from seeing the property you like to securing and finally settling on the property:

1. Visit land displays or read newspaper to have an idea of property prices or the price range.
2. Establish a good saving pattern- once you've acquired the knowledge about the property market and movement in property prices, establish a budget and stick to it. Track your expenses and cut back on expenditure. Make small sacrifices such as walking and using public transport to work instead of driving. Have a separate high interest account to save for the deposit (about $20,000) to avoid temptation of spending the money.
3. Set yourself a limit on saving for a deposit, such as six months to one year, but no longer than that. Get advice from a bank's financial planner or a broker.

4. Avoid taking out too many personal loans, car loans and credit cards. Your bank's financial planner or broker will be able to tell you about ways to reduce your personal loans such as debt consolidation and getting rid of all extra credit cards. These will decrease your borrowing capacity.
5. Buy outside the suburb where you live- if it is cheaper. You can later buy in your preferred area or buy now as an investment and a couple of years later move into that house.
6. Do not buy a house based on your feelings but on its capital growth potential and price (affordability). Buying an expensive 'nice' house could cost you the earth, especially if it is your home (PPOR), you're getting no tax deductions and you might later default on the loan.
7. Check future development- ask your local council about potential rezoning, infrastructure development such as schools and business developments such as shopping centres and residential schemes like apartment blocks or public housing. This information will determine the capital growth potential of your property.
8. Property design- ensure that the property is quality built and has quality fittings which will appeal to renters and give good valuation or capital growth over time.
9. Buy an investment to help pay off your PPOR- remember the aim of getting into the property market is not to own only one house as many people do and work the rest of their live to paying it off. It will cost you more this way. Consider buying an investment or two. A couple of years later, you can move into the investment for some six months (pay not capital gain tax) and sell it to pay

10. Check the capital growth rate of the last ten years- this will help to give a better indication of possible growth rate for the future.
11. Location- buy a house close to rivers, ocean, transport links and good facilities such as schools.
12. Understand the property cycle- this will ensure that you buy in the right cycle such as in a downturn instead of in a upswing/boom.

How I got started with only $2,000?

To invest you don't need a lot of cash. You can borrow from your house if you have one, to pay for upfront costs and the required deposit. I started investing in property with only $2,000 in my bank account. If you don't have a house, you can borrow as a personal loan and use the fund as a deposit with the same bank, or with a different institution. But your first property must be a good deal, giving you instant equity.

So, you can get started with very little or no money from your pocket. All you need is a full-time job. When the house is completed or increased in value, you can refinance the personal loan into the house. This is very important as a personal loan has higher interest rates charges than a home loan. This will reduce your borrowing capacity and affordability. For example, a $50,000 personal loan will require a repayment of about $1,000 per month. You can refinance that into the house and pay about $300 p/month. This gives you $700 per month in which you can quickly buy an investment which will increase in value. Afterwards it is just about managing cash flow and doing a bit of sacrifice.

Many home-buyers don't know how much they can afford to borrow and other basic lending details until they apply for a loan. If you can manage regular rent repayment, then it is possible that you can afford an average home ($300,000) that cost four to six times your gross (income before tax) annual income. Sometimes, you just have to add between $50-$100 a week on top of the rent you're currently paying. In the long run, it is better to pay a little extra more than the rent and buy your house rather than paying for someone else's mortgage.

For many people, the key to a good home loan is to save for a deposit of at least 20% to avoid lender's mortgage insurance. While this may be true, the fact is that very few people can save that much money. It will take you a long time to save. Time waited could be a loss of opportunity to get into the property market sooner and when prices are lower. Worse, property prices may have increased further above your initial deposit more while you've been saving, making all this effort fruitless.

Many institutions require only 5-10% deposit. Most lenders require a regular saving history but remember, I didn't have a good saving history and yet I was approved a loan. The key to home ownership is to have a job for more than 6 months that pays a decent wage rather than having a good saving record.

The bank will lend you money based on your financial commitments, your income, your credit history (no default such as phone bills) and job stability rather than your deposit. It is important to have a 'cash reserve' of at least three months to cover unexpected expenses. So, don't use all your saving on your first home, but keep some as a 'buffer' for a few months of repayment, and borrow the rest from your lender even if that means paying a bit of lender's mortgage insurance. That's why it is important to buy a cheaper home at first. It will be much easier to manage the expenses than buying a more expensive 'dream' home. This will enable you to buy your first investment much quicker.

Most lenders will lend about 30-40% of your total gross income on your home (PPOR) or your total loan commitments. For example, if your gross income is $1,200 a fortnight, your mortgage repayment should be about $500 a fortnight to fit most bank's debt servicing ratio (DSR). However, a $1,200 repayment on an investment doesn't mean that you have to contribute $1,200 yourself every month or that DSR is viewed the same way as the family home. Your rental income will be taken into account when calculating your DSR.

Why delaying investing will cost you a lot of money each year?

I was amazed when I got my first tax return of $4,000 and my wife got $2,500 in 2006, just because we built our first house and rented it out for one year while we were working up in the countryside in Western Australia. That was amazing, having a house that's growing in value, and using our taxes to pay for it. I wish I could have done this a long time ago. I was earning over $50,000 and paying about $13,000 in taxes. It was costing me over thousands of dollars every year by not investing.

My first property– PPOR:

I started investing in property in January 2005, by putting a deposit on a block of land in Mandurah while I was working as a high school teacher. I applied for a house and land package in January 2005.

How did I get the $14,000 for the deposit and establishment costs?

The broker came up with an innovative idea. I had a $15,000 personal debt ($11,000 car loan and $5,000 credit card) that I had to do pay off before I can apply for the home loan. I applied for a $20,000 personal loan and paid off the $16,000 debt and used the $4,000 leftover and my $2,000 saving as a deposit. With the $7,000 First Home Buyers Grant, I had $13,000 and was on my way to home–ownership. When the house was completed in October 2005, I refinanced the $20,000 personal loan into the home loan.

My first investment property-the property at Caversham.

The house was valued at $320,000 in November 2005, which meant I could borrow up to 90% of the equity from the house for an investment. In November 2005, I borrowed $25,000 from the home equity. I used $14,000 from the $25,000 to buy the block of land in Busselton ($124,000) and spent about $3,000 on fees such as stamp duty and mortgage insurance.

After I've placed a $1,000 deposit on the land and filling in the purchase paper, I bought an off-the-plan villa in Caversham which was to be completed in three months for $259,000. This was good as it brought in immediate rental income. I then approached St.George Bank to borrow the $165,000 for the building on the land in Busselton, but the bank refused.

I used the leftover money to finance the acquisition of the villa at Caversham in March 2006. However, with this new property rented by the end of the month, I was ready to refinance and borrow the money needed to start construction on the land at Busselton.

My second investment property (or 3rd property)-Busselton.
After being refused for the construction for the property at Busselton, I had to approach another bank for the loan. I contacted a mortgage broker at Wizard Home Loans. I refinanced the three loans (Caversham, PPOR and Busselton) with Wizard Home Loans and borrowed the extra $165,000 to complete construction of the house at Busselton.

My third investment property (4thproperty)-The Vines.
When I was negotiating the refinancing of the Busselton property I was also planning my fourth property purchase. I figured out that the sooner I can get more property the better. I saw a block of land in the newspaper at The Vines for $185,000. I knew the property at The Vines was a popular upmarket area. So, I negotiated a price reduction to $175,000 and put a $1,000 deposit on it with the real estate agent pending finance approval. I refinanced my home in Mandurah directly and borrowed $35,000 for the deposit on the land and borrowed the other $140,000. I could have negotiated the land for $160,000 but didn't.

Later, I approached a building company for construction and they have their own broker. I told the broker that I was an investor and that my bank has refused to lend me more money. I needed a smart broker to get the building loan for me. The broker refinanced this loan for me. So, I moved the $140,000 loan from St.George Bank to Westpac Bank, and borrowed an extra $148,000. The total loan was now $289,000. The cost for the building was only $130,000. The $30,000 I paid for the land was turned into a pre-approved top-up of $30,000. I had an extra $11,000 from the new loan of

$148,000 ($41,000 buffer in total). The $11,000 was deposited into my account. This was how I was able to acquire my fourth property. So, in September 2006, I had the loan for Busselton finalised and construction not long after. The property was ready to be rented in April 2007 and fetched $280 p/week in rent. Basically, I was able to acquire four properties in three years, from 2005-2007.

What I should have done instead?

I should have borrowed all the remaining equity from my PPOR and place it in a line of credit rather than increasing my home-loan directly.

Chapter 2-
Structuring your loan properly to borrow more money to expand your property portfolio and for asset protection.

Structuring your loan properly for growth:

It is important to establish the right structure for your loan from the start. After building or buying your first property, which is usually your PPOR to take advantage of the First Home Buyers Grant, borrow against it for investments. Banks tend to view the owner-occupier home as a strong security for they know people will do all they can to protect their home from repossession, even if that means giving up all luxuries.

The best way to structure your loan for growth include.

A- Set up a line of credit:

It is important to get a line of credit where you refinance and draw all the equity possible (watch for mortgage insurance) and place it in this account. This way your original home loan stays the same and the line of credit is a separate loan account. Then you will be in a position to use the line of credit to buy your first investment.

B- Establish interest only fixed loans:

It is best to set up interest only repayment on all your loans in the first five years, especially if cash is limited. This will free up cash for investment. It will also provide repayment certainty.

C- A combination of standalone and cross-securitised loans can be good:

Cross-securitised loans can be used when there is not enough equity in each property. Borrow money this way if your bank will be more willing to lend you more money. It is best to have standalone loans with lower LVR. Avoid cross-securitised your home (PPOR). This will give you more flexibility and control over your loan than cross-securitising your family home.

D- Spread your loans between two to three banks:

It is important to spread your loans with at least two lenders. This will keep you in control of your property. Once your loan reaches $1 million, you take on a different level of risk with your lender. They might not be willing to lend you more money, especially if you're borrowing with a high LVR. Always stay 'under banks radar' as much as possible. Be prepared to refinance and change bank if your bank simply rejects your loans. Avoid using a different institution for each loan as this will be too costly, complex and difficult to manage. Today, I have my loans with two banks.

E- Consolidate all personal debt:

To start investing in property, you don't have to be rich or have a lot of money in the bank. From my experience all you need is a full time job, knowledge and determination to succeed. When I started in property in 2005, I only had $2,000 in the bank, $5,000 credit card debt and $14,000 car loan. I had to consolidate and pay off my credit card and car loan by taking out one personal loan before I could apply for a home loan.

F- Using a personal loan as a cash deposit:

You can borrow the fund as a personal loan and use it as a deposit to buy your first property, either with the same bank or with a different bank. Do not tell the bank that you're going to use it as a deposit for a house as they might reject your loan. Just borrow for holidays or furniture. Then use it as a home deposit. That's all you need and this is how I got started.

If you're running short of money to keep the negatively geared properties, you can borrow as a personal loan say ($50,000) like I did in 2006, and then deposit the money in an offset account. You will pay about 14% in interest on the personal loan but will be getting a reduction in interest payment (7.5%) as the $50,000 in the offset account will reduce the loan balance. Basically you'll be paying only 6.5% interest on the $50,000 that can be a lifeline in bad times.

G- Borrowing from your house for a deposit-equity release:

You can borrow the equity from your properties as an equity release loan and use the money for a buffer fund or to buy another property.

H- Using an ABN to borrow below 80% LVR:

You can borrow 20% from an existing property and use the fund for a deposit on another property at an 80% LVR. This way you've borrowed a 100% for this new property or to top up the buffer fund.

I- Getting a tax variation:

Banks will calculate your loan repayments based on your income and will only include 75% of rental income. Getting a tax variation will increase your income each fortnight and improve your serviceability with the banks.

J- Redraw facility:

A redraw facility allows you to make additional loan repayments (be it investment or PPOR) which reduces the principal and interest rates repayment. You can access the money when needed. It is convenient and saves you money. Do not redraw the money unless you urgently need it and only use the money for investment purposes.

K- Offset account:

Set up an offset account to store surplus cash. Deposit all rental incomes and pays in this account linked to your house. The amount in the account will reduce the balance on your home loan and save you interests on the loan.

Investor's tip:

You don't need a lot of money to get started in property. You need to have the courage to take the risk and give it a go.

Why is the bank willing to lend money to property investors?

- **The banks understand the reliability of property investment as it delivers good returns to them and the investors.** They know that they can make billions by lending to investors.
- **Property offers security of 'bricks and mortar' to the bank:** it is the safest investment to the investors and the banks. If something goes wrong the bank has full control over the property.
- **Apart from investors:** the property market is dominated by mums and dads as owner occupiers. The banks know that they will do anything to protect their homes from repossession.
- **Consistent capital growth:** apart from the ups and downs of its normal cycle, property investment will deliver consistent capital growth over time. In fact, property has increased consistently over the last 1,200 years in the western world.
- **Income that grows:** cash flow from positively geared and commercial property.
- **Tax benefits:** you can claim interest repayments, loan application fees, borrowing costs, depreciation on assets, building cost write-off, council and water rates, insurance, property management fees, repairs and maintenance. This means that many investors will be able to afford their loan repayments.
- **You can borrow against it:** refinance standalone loans and/or cross-securitised property loans.

- **Lender's mortgage insurance-** LMI which you pay to protect the lender in case you default does also benefit you as it enables you borrow more than bank would otherwise lend you, up to 100% in some cases. If the proceeds from the sale of the property is not sufficient to cover the outstanding loan balance, the lender is able to claim any shortfall from the mortgage insurance company which they in turn sue/claim you to recover the balance. This reduces the lender's risk of taking a lower deposit and makes it possible for you to purchase a property with little deposit- a far cry from the 20% that was often required 20 years ago.
- **You don't have to sell to reap the benefits:** borrowing from existing property as a top up and a line of credit to live off or for renovations and other reasons and thus avoiding the costs (real estate agent fees, CGT) of selling a property to access cash.
- **Residential investment:** unlike a personal loan, which is mostly unsecured, residential property means that the bank has security over the house which they can repossess in case you default. Banks regard residential real estate as prime security, which they will lend up to 97% of the property's value, sometimes a 100%.
- **You can also leverage:** use a small amount of money to acquire an asset of a bigger value or borrow a large sum of money using a small amount of your own money. This means that banks are willing to lend you 19.5 times more than your deposit (5% deposit and borrow 95%) of the rest

of the money to buy a residential asset, on which you reap larger returns and growth over time. This is very important as otherwise only the rich would be able to afford to invest. Banks will allow you to leverage your investment so that the amount of money that you invest is low in relation to borrowing.

You have to use smart borrowing strategies to stay on top of your financial situation. Use funds from the line of credit for a deposit and borrow the rest of the money from a different institution. This way you have leverage of 100% and use the surplus funds in the line of credit to pay for establishment fees, and to cover the shortfall until the property increase in value. That's smart investment and leverage strategies. You have to be smart when dealing with the banks and use their money to help yourself. A line of credit is a good way to use bank money to leverage and buy property or build a buffer fund.

Investor's tip:
Don't try to save for a 20% deposit. Borrow 90-95% if you can. It is hard to save money and the property prices might have increased more than the saving while you wait.

According to statistics about 90% of investors rarely ever take the extra steps and risk to buy more than two investment property. Owning only one or two properties will not make a big difference to your life. You might not have a mortgage but you will still need to work. There is equity sitting in your house that you can safely use to your advantage. That's a waste of a great opportunity. Thousands of people in the western world are scared of taking on more debts. **The reasons are due to the :**

- fear of losing their family home and the investment properties they've acquired.
- fear of bankruptcy if they acquire too much debt.
- lack the courage to take the plunge.
- lack of knowledge of how to borrow money.
- lack of financial and property investment knowledge and the failure to understand the benefits of property investment which far outweigh working for a boss.
- inability to see beyond the income constraint.

The fact is that buying your first property is the hardest. People think that they need to save for that big deposit. But the reality is that you don't have to. This is because the government will help you such as a Home Buyers' Grant like in Australia. So, you don't have to save for the big deposit to put on your home (PPOR). You start to own your home sooner and use the money you're saving for the deposit to help finance the costs of an investment property, leaving extra cash for a 'rainy day.' You should borrow as much as possible from the bank when you start investing to claim the maximum tax deductions and have leftover money for your next investment. You can duplicate this process even on a limited income by using the equity in the property. My first broker told me a little secret of borrowing money even when your income limits your ability to borrow more money. He told me to set up an ABN. I discovered that getting an ABN or a business number (even if you're not running a business) as a property investor meant that you can borrow below 80% without declaring your income. This has two added benefits that can add fuel to the fire when it comes to accessing more funds to service your debt or buy more properties:

- You can borrow the 20% deposit for the deposit without having to prove your ability to service the loan or your income.
- You can use the 20% deposit from one institution and borrow the 80% from another. Thus, you've borrowed a total of 100% for the new property.
- You can also borrow 80% LVR for the investment as a no-doc loan. The bank will lend you money on the strength of the property. It's best to buy a property below market value and later revalue it and re-borrow the extra equity.
- Lender's mortgage insurance can be costly when it comes to accumulating more properties. That's why using an ABN is a good way of borrowing when not being able to show your income or serviceability. That's why 92% of investors accumulate only two investments. I bought four properties in three years without using an ABN. I can now use an ABN to borrow 80% LVR on a positively cash flow property which means borrowing and servicing the loan using no money from my pocket.

Investor's tip:

Check your credit rating with Veda Advantage if you live in Australia by calling 1300762207. For a small fee of $25 you can

get your file in a couple of hours be email or fax. For an annual fee of $25 you can monitor your credit file by having them notifying you by email every time a loan is registered on your file. This will guard against credit and identify fraud.

There are five ways to create a buffer of surplus cash to make your property cash flow positive now:

- Setting up a tax variation.
- Refinancing to set up spare cash in a line of credit.
- Setting up an offset account.
- Establishing a withdraw facility with your loan.
- Getting a professional depreciation schedule done on each of your property.

A- Increase the serviceability of your loans by getting a tax variation:

It is possible to inflate your income by getting a tax variation. You will have more money in your pay packet each pay day. This will improve your serviceability with the banks.

B- Spare cash in a line of credit:

By this, I mean have extra cash in a line of credit, especially if you have three properties like me. This will help you to sleep at night knowing that if something happens, you have money to protect your investments. Most investors think a buffer of at least 5-10% is necessary. Having a line of credit means that you can draw on it immediately without having to apply for a new loan. It is vital to borrow all the equity during boom times and use it during bad times such as a recession or if interest rates rises and you haven't fix your loans.

C- Setting up an offset account:

Deposit all rental incomes and your pays into the offset account. Offset account is similar to a withdraw facility in that it saves you interest on the amount in the account. Any surplus money in the account will reduce your interest payment each day. The more money there is in the account, the less interest you'll pay.

D- Redraw facility:

A redraw facility allows you to make additional loan repayments (be it investment or PPOR) which reduces the principal and interest bill. Better still, you can access the money when needed. A Withdraw facility is convenient and saves you money. Do not redraw the money unless you urgently need it or for investment purposes.

E- Get a professional depreciation schedule for all of your properties:

A depreciation schedule will add thousands of dollars in your pocket year after year for decades for a one off tax-deductible fee of $500. A $300,000 property can provide about $5,000 in tax deductions.

Chapter 3.
How to borrow more money to increase and accelerate your property portfolio without declaring your income?

Borrow money using an ABN as a no-doc loan:
What can you do when you don't less than 20% equity in your properties and your income limits your ability to borrow more money?
You can borrow money using an ABN by borrowing below 80% LVR. You can borrow 20% of the deposit from an existing property or from your line of credit and use the fund for a deposit on another property at an 80% LVR. This way you will not have to declare any income (no-doc loan) and pay no lender's mortgage insurance. You don’t need to have a business to have an ABN.

What does a 'no doc loan' look like?

A 'no-document loan' is a very important way of raising finance to invest in more properties. When income becomes a problem and you cannot afford any more properties or cannot demonstrate your serviceability, 'no document loan' becomes very handy. It is important that you plan ahead as you need to have the business number for at least two years before you can use it to borrow money.

Lender's mortgage insurance can be costly when it comes to accumulating more properties. That's why the majority of property investors accumulate only two investments. That's why using an ABN is a good way of borrowing. I didn't know much about ABN when I first started into property investment.

If you live in Australia, setting up an ABN is vital as is can be the fastest way to grow your portfolio. All you have to do is go to this website: www.ABR.com or the ATO www.ATO.gov.au. Just fill out the ABN form online or print and fax to ATO. Also, call ATO and register for GST. It's that easy. On the form declare that you are a property investor. You only pay GST if you are constantly buying and selling property or actively running a business. When you get the GST letter from the tax office, state that you are not currently traded. You will need a good broker, who is also an investor and familiar with 'no-doc' loan to help you apply for one.

You can borrow the 80% fund for the property with the same bank you've borrowed the 20% deposit or with a different bank. This is because if you borrow all the funds from one institution, that institution might say that you cannot service the new debt. This will only happen if you have a lot of debts with that institution. The bank where you're borrowing the other 80% fund will not normally challenge you as you're borrowing below their safety zone of 80% LVR. That bank also have security over the property.

Borrowing using an ABN (business number) or a no-doc loan explained. There is a 4 page document to be signed.

Page 1- a loan application fees schedule:

You need to pay the valuation fee and mortgage broker's fees upfront. These fees are tax deductible but not-refundable. It will cost you about $500 in broker's fee and $300-$600 for valuation fee for each property being used in the loan application.

Page 2-3- an individual self-certified declaration low/no doc loan affordability documentation:

These pages say 'do not complete or declare your income if it is a no-doc loan.' This is a loan affordability declaration or self-certifying your ability to repay the loan. You just need to sign and date the two pages.

Page 4- is a permission to obtain information about your credit history from credit reporting agencies:

You must sign this page which gives the lender permission to obtain personal information from your credit file. The loan application is complete. The bank property valuers will call you to gain access to your properties for valuation. No income check will be conducted.

Below is my loan application where I refinanced three of my

properties to create a buffer fund.

Loan application: Name of applicant (s):

Loan amount: $955,000 which will pay out existing loans of:

1. Mandurah- $278,000.
2. The vines- $288,000.
3. Caversham- $289,000.
4. Short term funding 'buffer'- $100,000.

Total security/equity of $1,190,000, consisting of:

5. Mandurah- $430,000.
6. Caversham- $360,000.
7. The Vines- $400,000.

This means that my LVR is below 80%. If valuation comes lower than that, I can borrow less, let's say, $75,000 instead of $100,000. Property valuation is very important here.

Investor's tip:

Re-value the properties and borrow the equity for a deposit on your next purchase or to top up your buffer fund. Watch out for serviceability by buying very slightly negatively geared or positively geared properties only.

Part 4-
Investing in real estate and understanding the property market.

Chapter 1.
Good practical advice for first time investors.

Important advice when buying a property investment:

1. Research and gain a solid understanding of the property value and possible growth prospect of the type of property that you're buying. Comparable sales and possible valuation reports are available on-line for a small fee.
2. Don't borrow more than you can repay. Do the sum first and buy a cheaper property if you need to. Stick to your borrowing limit regardless of what the lender offers you.
3. Negotiating your purchase price: be prepared to negotiate on the price of the property. Don't rush when making a decision.
4. Building inspection: always get a pest and building inspection on the property before you buy. It will cost around $500.

When buying:

1. Avoid taking advice from anyone who has a vested interest in the

property they're selling you. Educate yourself so that you won't be ripped off. Spend time getting to know your advisor's first before using their advice.

2. Purchase the property only after you've researched the area thoroughly. It's good to access the growth history and sales data of the property market. Visit website: www.myrpdata.com.au or www.residex.com.au for up-to-date data on property prices, predicted capital and rental growth.
3. Buy in growth suburbs.
4. Building equity: adding an extra room which will add substantial value to the property and some people even rent a back room of their house.
5. Don't try to save for a 20% deposit. Borrow 90% if you can instead of waiting to save for the deposit.
6. Set yourself a buffer for unexpected expenses and future plans. Have a long-term goal for property investment.

Planning to invest in property:

1. Set an investment goal and educate yourself about property investing and stick to your plan. Buy books and magazines to read.	5. Save some money each pay day to invest in property. This will create wealth and enable you to retire earlier. Make an effort to save at least 10-20% of your income each pay-day for a deposit on an investment property.
2. Make sacrifices and give up something to achieve this.	6. Factor in on top of the purchase price, about 5-10%

	extra for stamp duty, government charges, settlement fees, mortgage insurance and bank fees.
3. Look for affordable properties.	7. Look for cash flow or near cash flow properties. Make this your hobby.
4. Attend free property seminars to keep up-to-date with property investment news.	8. Keep up-to-date with the tax laws in regard to property investment in your country.

Investor's tip:
Always borrow extra in a line of credit as a 'buffer' to help pay interest or the shortfall until the property increases in value or pay for itself. Make sure that you have the proper insurance in place to protect your assets.

Other practical advice:
1. Research and negotiate with your lender for a better deal. It is important to monitor the market regularly to stay up-to-date with new products. There are many lenders both banks and non-bank lenders who are keen to get your business. Examine your current loan and compare it to that of other lenders. If you've received a pay rise since taking out the loan, ask your lender for a better deal or if they can match what's on offer in the market.

2. Pay extra on your home loan. The fastest way to pay off your home (PPOR) is to make extra repayments and pay fortnightly rather than monthly. Even $100 per fortnight will save thousands and cut years off your home loan (PPOR).

3. Reduce your spending habits. Make small changes to your spending and saving patterns to ease pressure on your finances. For example, take lunch to work instead of buying and cancel the gym membership and work out at home.

4. Reduce credit cards debt. Switch to a 0% interest balance transfer for six-nine months. Look for one with a lower interest rate or 55 days interest free period. Use it to pay all your bills and pay off the balance in full before payment is due. Use it with an offset account linked to your home loan.

5. Don't be attracted by low interest loans. Look at the total cost of borrowing (comparison rates). Get a broker to work that out for you. Some low rates are achieved through higher account keeping, redraw, monthly and annual fees.

6. Check your home loan statements. Human and even computer errors are responsible for mistakes in your home loan, costing you thousands of dollars. Make sure that you're being charged the right amount and right interest rates. Buy a software called " Mortgage watchdog" for $180. Visit: **www.mortgagewatchdog.com**. **If you detect any errors contact your lender.**

Important advice to property investors:

1. You need to have a good budget: if you're a committed investor who wants to create wealth and achieve financial freedom. You will need to keep track of your income and expenditure. Cut back on unnecessary items such as pay TV and dining out. A budget becomes critical in times of rising interest rates.

2. Get a tax variation now if it is necessary. Do not spend it on your living expenses.

The basic principles of property investing:

1. **Have patience:** property is a long term investment of at least 7-10 years commitment.
2. **Keep emotions out of it:** don't buy the property because you like it or your friends or property seminars presenters say you should. You won't be living in the property.
3. **Maximise your tax:** claim all tax deductions and depreciation entitlements which can be about 80% of the property total purchase price (new property).
4. **Set reasonable rent:** charge affordable rent and don't be greedy. You want tenants that will be happy to rent for a while and keep the property in good condition.
5. **Set money aside for property improvements and maintenance:** a poorly maintained property will give your property a lower valuation when you have the property valuated.
6. **Set goals on what you want to do with your investment:** are you going to buy more properties or just maintain what you have?
7. **You must have financial discipline:** it is important to set aside money to maintain the property, especially if it is negatively geared.
8. **Use a good professional real estate manager:** the property

manager will look after the property for you.

9. **Calculate or have an idea of capital growth before you invest:** you're investing for profit.

Table 1- good money management tips:

A. Make sure that you use a good broker. If you want to approach the bank yourself, choose a bank that offers a good interest rate and no monthly fees. A well-established broker will have all the information and more negotiating power with the banks than you.
B. Fix your loan at a good rate and wait. This will ensure certainty of repayment when interest rates increase.
C. Split your loan (part fix and part variable). Thus, you will be protected against interest rate rises and have access to loan features such as line of credit and offset account. That is the best of both worlds. You can fix 80% of the loan and leave 20% variable, linked to an offset account. You can then make extra repayment on this loan (PPOR) rather than on your investment loan.
D. You can choose to make fortnightly payment instead of monthly, as this will add two extra repayments per year and save money on interest. You can have access to this fund from the withdrawal account if you urgently need it.
E. Get a package on your home loan. This will give you a discount on your loan and reducing interest rates. I have a professional package loan with Wizard Home Loans and one with Westpac Bank, with a $5,000 credit card limit.
F. Deposit all rents and salary into an offset account. Use your

credit card for your daily expenses and pay off the balance before the interest free period expires. This will save you interest for the time your money stays in the offset account. The offset account is a good way to make your money work harder. The key is to avoid getting a big credit card, as this will get you into trouble.
G- Bargain with the lender in regards to variable interest rates, upfront and ongoing fees. You can shop around for the best deal. Make sure that your demands are realistic.
H- Use the Internet to make comparisons between their interest rates, features, upfront and ongoing fees. Once you've done your research, you can approach the bank and they will take you seriously. Remember, do your negotiations face to face to exert the maximum pressure on the bank and never give up easily.

Effective money management.

Planning to live off the rental income and capital growth.

1. You need to repay the debt, especially on your PPOR. Repaying just a few dollars each pay day will reduce your interest bill and get rid of the debt on your non-tax deductible asset (PPOR) sooner than and saves you thousands in interest.

2. Making additional repayments in a withdrawal account to keep your interest bill down.

3. Selling one or two properties, and using the excess cash to pay debts on the rest of the investment properties. Keep some spare cash and invest in assets that don't have a lot of expenses such as shares and commercial property which will bring additional returns. It is best to sell the asset in year when you're not working

or working part-time.

4. After acquiring all the properties you want and you're ready to work less, you can start to reduce your debts and live off the increasing equity and rental income. Borrow against the properties by borrowing below 80% LVR, using an ABN for living expenses. This way you can have six investment properties remaining which are all cash flow positive, live in a house (PPOR) which I own outright.

5. Even low income workers can get ahead financially and amass a fortune over time. It takes persistence, planning and sacrifice, but it can be done. You need to spend more on investment than on designer clothes, flash cars and holidays.

How to better manage your cash flow?

Keep investment (tax-deductible) loans and PPOR (non-tax deductible) loan separate:

When it comes to doing your tax, it is important to keep your PPOR and for personal expenses account and investment loans separate. It will be very complicated if you use the same account for both. Otherwise, you and your accountant will have to apportion the tax deductible expenses and this can be difficult and time consuming. To protect your interest deductibility but still get the benefits of a line of credit account, set up an offset account linked to your loan. Now use the line of credit only for investment purposes such as paying interest. Use the offset account to draw funds for private purposes.

As an investor it is crucial to cover yourself for anything that can go wrong. A line of credit is an extension of your existing loan which you can draw on as you need it. Some banks charge the same interest rate or 0.25% more on their line of credit as their standard variable home loan rate. You might lose your job, tenants might damage the property and it might need repairing or a severe recession can leave the property without a tenant for a while and consequently, no rental income.

You need to be prepared before these events happen. I did prepare for everything except rising interest rates. As long as interest rates is low and stable, property investors don't have to worry.

My mistakes were three-folds:

1. Not setting up a big line of credit at the start of my journey into property investing.2. Not fixing my interest rates for at least three years when I had the chance, to protect against rising interest.

3. Not setting up an ABN for my property and register for GST.

Ways to reduce your mortgage repayments.

Interest rates will have a big influence on property values, ease of property accumulation and capital gains as they directly affect the affordability and holding costs of property. It will also reduce your borrowing capacity. There are other ways to reduce your repayment:

1. Look for a better deal: ask your lender to match what's on offer at different institutions and give you a better deal. Refinance if your lender is not keen to help but only if the discharge fees and establishment fees are reasonable or can be recovered within a year. You're entitled to a refund on your mortgage insurance if you refinance that loan within two years of setting it up.

2. Get a professional package loan: if the total loans are more than $250,000, you can get a discount on your standard variable rate. The bigger the loan, the more will be the discount. I've received a discount of 0.6% on my loans with Wizard Home loans and Westpac Bank.

3. Use an experienced mortgage broker: they can negotiate with the lender on your behalf at no cost to you.

4. Research: use the internet to look for finance good deals on offer. Visit: www.cannex.com.au.

5. Split your rates: when rates are low, split your rate, to protect against rate rises and have flexibility of features such as 100% offset account.

6. Consolidate your debts: since interest rate discounts are largely based on your total borrowings, moving all your loans with two lenders will increase your negotiating power.

Investor's tip:

Calculate how much the property is going to cost you before and after tax and the potential capital growth prospect before you invest.

Chapter 2-

Location, location, location. Where to buy for optimum growth and income? How to pick a good property?

Why location is important for profitable returns from property investment?

You need to spot places that have booming potential.

Location is an important consideration to include in your calculation before you invest. You must invest in certain areas which have the potential to grow quickly. When we hear about property investing in the media, we are primarily looking at the popularity, the rental and capital growth prospects of the place. Property investors look for property that will make them wealthy and rich quickly. It is hard to make $20,000 extra cash profits each year in rental growth but you can make $20,000 in capital growth, if you've bought in the right location. Rental income will also increase but at a slower pace. When we say that there is a property boom, most of the time we are referring to certain areas growing well rather than the whole country booming. Some areas will achieve great capital growth or price increases while others will grow very slightly and others stagnant. This growth area occurs due to location.

The best way to make money in real estate investment is to pinpoint a hotspot before it becomes popular. There are observable factors/qualities responsible for this. I built my first home in Mandurah for obvious reasons.

A- First stage of land release.

The land was in the first stage of land release. First stage of land release is always cheaper than subsequent stages of land releases in the housing estate. Consequently, construction cost will be cheaper and increase as activities intensify. So, getting early in the frenzy is important. I knew that $83,000 was cheap for a 540sqms block in Mandurah, a popular crabbing and fishing place. It has all the facilities of a growing town. Today, this same block of land is worth about $250,000. You cannot find any block of land for under $150,000.

B- Sea change and lifestyle features.

Mandurah has all of these features. People are attracted to living by the ocean, especially those approaching retirement. This factor will increase property value in an established area.

C- Transport and other infrastructure.

New rail lines and road links can add value to properties close or along the transport routes. A new road will open up previously inaccessible areas or provide faster connections and communications for commuters to the city. New roads or highways open up the bush area for property development and will boost property values along suburbs close to the road and rail lines. Check with your local council, government land department, and real estate institute about planned developments.

D- Urban renewal and governments projects.

State and local governments can transform an area. Urban renewal programs will change the appearance and appeal of the old 'ugly ducklings' into 'a beautiful swan.' This will increase property values in a short-time as more people will rush in to invest there. Keep up-to-date and buy in the first stage of land release. New port, marina and residential apartment development are good examples.

E- Mining projects.

Developments such as mining and industrial projects will attract people (workers and families) to the area and create a mini-boom. Places with new mining and industrial projects are excellent areas to invest before the boom.

F- Location.

The better the location of the property in terms of access to good infrastructure such as public transport, services such as child care, shopping centres, medical centres, schools and employment will increase its value and attract a good tenant. That property is likely to double in value in about 7-10 years. The nicer the area the greater the possibility of capital growth on the investment in the future.

Property buying tips:

The property or area must have good rental potential.

1) Buy the property below market value and avoid older property where you have to do extensive work.
2) Buy as close to the land value as possible as you want to make money on the purchase cost as well as the sale price or growth value.
3) Buying the 'worst house in the best street' is better than buying 'the best property in the worst suburb' as location is the key to property growth.
4) Find out by doing research at real estate offices, local and national offices if the property prices for the area are going up or not.
5) Buy in areas where there are planned or actual new infrastructure developments such as new shopping centres, railways, free-ways and marinas.
6) Buy within 10 to 15 kilometres from the city to gain instant equity or have good growth prospect.
7) Where there is a growing population, new industries and employment.
8) Where there is a lot of leisure facilities, lifestyle choices and near a river or ocean.
9) Choose a property larger than 50 square metres and medium sized land of at least 450 square metres.
10) Buy renovated property with good designs.

There are lots of places to buy for optimum growth and income. The most important point is to ensure that:

- You don't pay too much for the property.
- You are not too highly geared and can afford the mortgage repayments..
- There are a lot of economic activities in the area and the area has been earmarked for development or redevelopment.
- The place is becoming very popular with families moving into the new houses.
- The properties will be cash flow neutral or near that when all tax deductions are added.

How to pick a good property from the thousands on the market?

1. Look at sales history:

Look at the sales history of the area and the capital or price increases of the property compared to when it was first built. This will give you a better idea of whether this is a good property to buy or not. Check to see that the property market is not 'over-heating.' This happens when the market of an area has achieved an excellent growth in a short period of time, for example, 50% growth in one year.

2. Rental demand:

The second factor driving property growth is rental demand. Choose in places where there's a strong rental demand which means that property prices will rise due to scarcity. Population growth with people from other states or overseas will increase rental income.

Table - market value check-list	Yes	No
Are there any development planned for		

the area?		
Have you done an independent valuation?		
Have you checked the sale figures for similar, minimum, maximum and average property prices?		
Has the been good capital growth for the area over the past five years?		
Is the property on the main road or in a secure or under-cover parking?		
Have you talked to your local real estate agent about sales prices for houses and units?		

To better predict the booming potential of a location you need to:

1. Look at the sales history: if you buy a property where there has been a history of sales in the past and present, there is a great chance that the area will grow in the future.
2. Rental demand: will accelerate property growth. Choose in places where there's a strong rental demand which means that property prices will rise due to excess demand.

These factors are important in selecting a good property:

- A lot of building activity.
- Close to the city or town with lots of leisure facilities and lifestyle choices. A lot of new infrastructure, new industries and employment.
- Near a river or ocean.
- Choose a property larger than 50 square metres, on medium sized land and new or renovated property with good design and quality fittings.
- Growing population.

These factors affect the growth rate of property:

1. There is a lot of building activity, be it government infra-structures such as road and railways. New housing development, especially in the early stages of land release is good as the land is still cheaper and price increases as more land is released.
2. Where there are a lot of private investments and development such as new shopping centres. Make sure that there is good infrastructure where your property is located. Facilities such as road, schools, hospitals and recreation are important.

3. Where there is employment or new industries. This will attract workers and their families to the area and there will be rental demand. Income growth is also a factor in capital growth.
4. Where there is a new housing estate with growing population who will rent your property. A place where there's strong population growth and limited capacity for increased supply will lead to scarcity and price increases. The next decade will be good for property investors as was in the last 10 years. Immigration and interstate migration in Australia will boost the population of places like Perth and in Queensland due to lifestyle factors. Wages and rent will have to keep pace with increasing property values.
5. Close to the city, at least 20 kilometers from it as it will be easy for people to commute. It is best to buy closer to the city or town, within a radius of 20 kilometers. This is because people, especially new arrivals like to live close to the city as they like the facility and lifestyle.
6. There are a lot of leisure facilities and lifestyle choices such as gym and schools. Recreational facilities and good schools will attract families. Select properties in good suburbs and one with a history of capital growth and high demand, especially with owner-occupiers. Tenants will be able to afford the rent and more willing to pay the higher rent.
7. Near a river or ocean if you can afford where land is limited. More and more houses are being built further away from the beach. Buying/building close to rivers and oceans will give you greater capital growth to accumulate more properties than in a regional area. It is also easier to rent the property.

8. Choose a property larger than 50 square metres and medium sized land. As more Australian chooses to have less kids and work longer hours, a property with about 450 square metres will be suitable for future families with fewer kids.
9. Property with good design. Well-built homes will appeal to renters and they will be willing to pay higher rent for it. I prefer new properties as most renters like living in a new home and will look after it better than an older style home.
10. Areas undergoing urban renewal will see increase property values in the future. The new port marina and residential development are good examples. New mining and industrial projects are excellent areas to invest before the boom.

Why picking a good location is important for profitable returns from property investment?

Your aim as an investor is three-folds:

- Achieve good capital growth in the next 7 years.
- For the property pay for itself as soon as possible.
- Make the property put money into your pocket.

The better the location in terms of access to good infrastructure such as public transport, services such as child care, shopping centres, medical centres, schools and employment, the greater the chance that the property will increase in value and attract a good tenant. That property is likely to double in value in about 10 years. The nicer the area, the greater the possibility of capital growth on the investment in the future. There is no point in buying just any property at a high price if you're going to lose lots of money in the hope that in the end the property will be worth a lot more. What if the property value doesn't materialise because of wrong location?

Investor's tip:
Town-houses, villas and houses are good investments due to the land content. Also, future renters will require smaller houses on smaller lots with good security and low maintenance. Apartments close to the city or close to water and of decent sizes are excellent investment, but make sure that you don't overpay for them.

What's the best type of property to buy?
1. Houses:
I find it a better investment to buy a house rather an apartment unless the apartment is quite big, in a well-located area and in limited supply, like in Mandurah waterfront apartments. Always buy below the market/property valuation to give you a buffer in case the market retracts or the market book and presents you with opportunity for a bargain. However, houses tend to have the highest capital growth compare to town-houses and apartments. That's why all my investments are house. I find that houses tend rise faster in value than units. This is because land increase in value and buildings depreciate.

Investor's tip:
You should always consider the land content of your investment as it is land that is in short supply and will increase in value over time and make you wealthy.

Table- house check-list	**Yes**	**No**
Are there any development planned for the area?		
Is it a well-looked after area and does it have a good transport route and infrastructure?		
Are buyers and tenants moving there in great numbers?		
Is it close to the sea, river and city?		
Is the house near the airport or major free-ways or roads?		

2. Units/Apartments:

An apartment close to the ocean and rivers and the city centre can be a good investment but they must be more than 50sqm and at least two to three bedrooms. Research has shown that apartments suffer the most when the market retracts, especially units in a high rise. It is hard to sell in a falling market as there will be an excess supply of apartments. Remember scarcity is what makes a property attractive and add value.

Remember, new apartments in my opinion is better than old ones. For example, there are new apartments in Mandurah in Western Australia. These are good investment due to scarcity. They are close to the water and there is a limited amount of land close to the sea in Mandurah in the vicinity of the town. Do your research, evaluate the property and do not pay too much. Now is the time to buy as the market is in a downturn. Always bargain and if you buy off-the-plan, buy the first lot of apartment release. Bargain if you can and research the capital growth possibility of the place and tenant vacancy rate.

Apartments in Perth and a new development in a suburb called Burswood and Ascot are good investments, because they are close (5 minutes) to the city. Land close to the city, like these are limited in supply. These units will cost you extra for strata fees and lift maintenance. If you're buying a unit, buy one with good access to infrastructure and transport and pick one in a small complex.

Table- unit check-list	**Yes**	**No**
Are there any development planned for the area?		

Is the unit in a safe, well-light and well-maintained area. Is it near good transport route and infrastructure?		
How much is the strata fees?		
Are there more owner-occupiers than renters in the complex and in the vicinity?		
Is parking available for tenants?		
Are the properties on the main road or in a secure and or under-cover parking?		
Does the unit have internal facilities such as shared gym, pool, and washer?		
Have you talked to your local real		

estate agent about recent sales prices/figures for units?		

3. Villa in a small complex:

Villas can be a good investment due to the land content and the fact that future Australian renters will require smaller house on smaller lot with good security and low maintenance. I prefer of villas in a small complex as it is easier to rent and maintain. My villa in Caversham in Western Australia, which is about 20 minutes to the city, is in a small block of 8 units and land content of 275sqm.

Investor's tip:

Invest in high growth areas as property investment is a low risk and high growth investment. But you need to choose carefully.

Importance of negotiating with builders and land sales agents:

The other mistakes I made was not negotiating with building contractors when I was building the property at Busselton. I blew my budget by $25,000. It cost me $165,000 to build the house. I later realised that I paid too much for the house, it was a smaller house (150sqm) on 639 square metres block and it was not the best design. I could have got a better design and a bigger house and much cheaper if I've shopped around and used a different builder. The house would have cost me $140,000, a saving of $25,000. That's why it is important to do a bit of research and bargain a bit with the construction company. I didn't, but just accepted the price they gave me and didn't fully investigate the design of the house. You need to get as many quotes from many builders before making a final decision on which builder to choose from. Ask them to send you brochures of the house design with price and all features of the house included. They will ask you for land size and possible house size you need to build on the land. All councils have limit on house size for the size of land. They might ask you about your budget, always give them a budget lower than what you plan to spend. This way you will be bargaining hard for saving, and saving equal equity. For example, if you have a budget of $170,000 to build the house, tell them you only have $140,000 to spend.

Borrow an extra, say $30,000 for landscaping and general works. A total budget $200,000 loan pre-approval. This way you let them come to the party and bargain hard. In the end, ensure that it cost you less than what the bank has agreed to lend you, so that you have money ($30,000) to complete the backyard and the cross-over. There is extra money to cover for the loan repayments during construction.

Part 5-
How to make money fast in real estate-gearing and leverage.

Chapter 1-
Understanding leverage and gearing- the key to wealth creation and how to increase cash flow.

It is important to know if your property investment will be cash flow positive or negatively geared before you invest.

What is gearing?

Gearing is the result of your investments. Some countries such as Australia, UK and New Zealand allow a tax deduction for property investors who make losses on their rental properties.

There are three types of gearing:

- **Positively geared**: asset making a profit.
- **Negatively geared**: asset losing money.
- **Neutrally geared**: asset paying for itself.

A- Negative gearing:

Although negative gearing can help you initially with the costs of your expenses and shortfall while you wait for capital and rental growth, you have to ensure that your losses are kept to a minimum. You must be able to afford these losses. The annual losses must be less than the yearly capital growth. You should also ensure that this loss is short-term, of at least five years.

Table 1- a negatively geared investment looks like this:

Rental income:	$20,000
Other property expenses	$18,000
Depreciation benefits	$6,000
Total rental expenses	$24,000
Net rental loss:	$4,000 loss
Tax saving:	

This is called negative gearing as the investor is making a net rental loss of about $4,000 per year.

The advantages of negative gearing:

- Offsetting your short-term losses against your income tax paid or other incomes.
- Reducing your tax bill while at the same time creating wealth for yourself.

- Increasing your wealth from borrowing large sums of money to invest in property and claiming all the costs and temporary loses against your incomes.
- Using your taxes to create and accelerate your wealth creation (tax saving).
- The greater your investment and losses, the greater will be your tax deductions. If you make $30,000 property losses before tax, your taxable income will be reduced by that amount and thus reducing your tax bill or increasing your tax refund.
- The higher your tax rate, the higher will be your tax rate deductions. For example, a person on a $200,000 income and on the highest tax bracket/rate (45%), will generally get a higher tax deduction on their losses compared to someone on a $45,000 income and a 10% tax rate.
- Your capital growth is not taxed.

The disadvantages:

- You can't claim more deductions than the tax you've paid. If you've paid $20,000 in taxes and make $20,000 in property losses, you cannot get all this $20,000 back, only part of it.
- You generally only get a tax refund based on your tax rate. Your taxable income will be reduced by the amount of the losses. You will be taxed on this lower income taxable income but rarely will you get a tax refund equal to your losses.

B- Positive gearing:

Positive gearing is very important and it should be the ultimate aim off all property investors. Positive gearing when mixed with negative gearing with capital growth, can be the best strategy of increasing your wealth quickly. Positive income can be used to finance and buy more properties, pay off the debt and make you rich (cash rich). Capital growth will make you wealthy. Remember with positively geared properties, you are using all tax deductions/expenses possible to reduce the tax payable on the rental profits. The larger the excess or positive income, the more taxes you will pay on this positive income. When you have positive cash flow properties, you will try to keep as much of the excess rental income in your pocket as possible. Depreciating deductions will be very important to help reduce your tax liability.

Table 2- a positively geared investment looks like this:

Rental income:	$28,000
Other property expenses	$18,000
Depreciation benefits	$6,000
Total rental expenses	$24,000
Net rental profit:	$4,000 +

Tax liability/saving:	

The property is said to be cash flow positive by $4,000.

The benefits of positive gearing:

- You are not contributing anything from your pocket to keep the property.
- You are making money each year from the property.
- These positive incomes will keep on rising each year if you've fixed your interest rates.
- There is capital growth that is yours to keep.
- You pay no tax on your capital gains each year unless you sell the property.
- Surplus income can be used to pay off existing debts.
- Income to live off and finance your lifestyle.
- Income to make you richer.

The disadvantages:

- Your taxable income will increase and your profits will be taxed.
- You will pay more tax and get a lower tax refund. Sometimes you will get no tax refund and maybe a tax bill on your rental profits unless you've prepaid interest 12 months in advance.

Turning negative gearing into positive cash flow.

It is important to know that over time, rental income would begin to exceed tax deductions. Your property will become positively geared or cash flow positive. This is the aim of investing, as it means that the property is paying for itself and making a profit.

Common ways how this can happen by:

- Decreased interest repayments.
- Rent increases more than interest repayments.
- Claiming all depreciation benefits.
- Getting a tax variation and setting up a short-term buffer fund.

So, what have been the benefits of property investing for me?

1. Increased equity and capital growth.
2. Increased rental income.

Which is better: cash flow positive investment with slow capital growth or negatively geared property with capital growth?

I think that a combination of negatively geared and positively geared cash flow properties is better than having all negatively or all positively cash flow properties. It's like mixing cordial, the positively geared properties provide funds to cover the shortfall of the negatively geared properties. The capital growth on the negatively geared properties enable you to borrow the equity to buy more properties and provide for a buffer fund. That is the only way you can acquire and service the increasing good debt without losing money. If you can buy or build positive cash flow properties with good capital growth, then you're on the road to financial freedom faster.

Once you've bought 3-4 negatively geared properties you are breaking even. If you buy another negatively geared property, you will be losing money. You will have to dig from your saving to service the debt. This will cost you too much in the long run. Every now and then you can buy a negatively geared property to add to your portfolio. This will increase your wealth and equity that you can tap into to buy the next property or cover the shortfall, if necessary. So, a combination of both is better.

Investor's tip:
You should buy a combination of some slightly negatively geared properties with good capital growth and some positive geared cash flow properties.

Let's see the importance of capital growth to an average investor:

Borrower No.1-Paul.

Paul and his wife had built their first home (PPOR) in 1999 for $200,000. They only have about $20,000 cash saving and figured out that they need another $20,000 for house deposit plus about $5,000 for other establishment cost. They did not want to pay lender's mortgage insurance if they borrow about 80% LVR which they pay to protect the lender if they default on the loan and not them. So, they decided to borrow $25,000 as a short-term personal loan. When the house was completed in the year 2000, they refinanced this $25,000 into the house to reduce their repayments. Their new debt on the house was now $185,000. In 2001, the couple decided to get an investment property. They approached a broker or lender for pre-approval. The property was valued at $400,000 and that's about $215,000 worth of equity the couple had in the house. Preparing to acquire his first investment, Paul did an equity release from his house and borrowed $100,000 in a new line of credit. Paul has been reading books about property investing and researching for an investment property for more than a year now. Paul bought an investment property in 2001. A 5 year old house, with 4 bedrooms and 2 bathrooms. It was in excellent condition close to infrastructure, such as roads, schools and shops. He did a valuation on the property before buying and after some hard bargaining bought the property at 20% below its value as the owners were keen to sell and move into a brand new property elsewhere. It was valued at $420,000 and Paul bought it for $340,000. He instantly got $80,000 equity outright. That's instant capital growth. After a prior chat with a real estate agent, he found out that those types of property were getting over $360 per week in rent, as it was close to a big shopping centre and a good and reputable private school.

He was quite knowledgeable about property investment having attended many free seminars on this subject. He visited an accountant to work out his tax entitlements and a broker to get a loan pre-approval letter before going shopping for the property. As the finance pre-approval letter lasted for three months, Paul had a bit of time to bargain for a good discount on the property. That property has been on the market for a while, as the property market was in a slowdown. The owner has over-priced his property for the market conditions. Paul knew after talking to the real estate agent selling the property that the owner cannot hold on to the property for too long, as he has bought another house elsewhere. Otherwise they will have two mortgages to pay.

So, Paul held on to his bid, increasing it very slightly until the owner accepted it. Well done, Paul. Paul immediately hired a property manager and rented the property for $340 per week. He chose to rent it cheaply to attract a suitable and reliable tenant as soon as possible. A property vacant for too long is not good. This is because you're losing money in two ways: missed rental income and paying advertising costs. So, the property was rented within two weeks. In the meantime, he was also researching for a cash flow property, or a property with good growth potential but slightly negatively geared, below $5,000 of property losses a year.

Since, he was only earning just an average income of $70,000 per year, Paul's properties need to be slightly negatively geared or near cash flow positive. He has to keep his losses to a minimum. If his loses on the two properties rise, he will need to contribute more from his pocket to maintain them.

He has placed his tenant on a 12 months lease, with a rent review every six months. He wanted a good and stable tenant. He figured out that a minimum rent increase of $10-15 per week, every six-month was needed to keep pace with inflation. Paul realised that as his wife was only working part time and looking after their little child, the property has to be fully in his name for maximum tax deductions.

Paul was comfortable with the loan repayment and fixed it for 5 years at 6.5% interest only. The variable rate was about 6%, but

Paul realised that he bought the property at the bottom of the property cycle since the last boom was seven years ago. The property market has slowed and even went backwards for about three years now. He knew after reading books on property investment, that the property market will eventually recover and a boom must be at least three years away. He has heard of the media starting to talk positively about property investment.
He was now in search for another property to realise great capital growth when the next boom takes place. So, six months after buying his first property, Paul bought another three bedroom and two bathroom house on a 550 square metres block. It was 20 kilometres from the city centre but in a growing suburb. Paul had it valued before buying, and it came up to $380,000. He paid $320,000 for it. That's $60,000 in instant equity. He immediately hired a property managing agent to advertise and manage the property. Over two weekends, the couple painted the house. They installed new curtains, new tiling and laminate flooring. Paul rented a hotel room for four nights and recorded the kilometres travelled in his log book. He knew that all the expenses for the two nights will be fully tax deductible. Paul rented the property for $350 per week and fixed his interest rates at 6.75% for five years as interest only. Paul's property education has paid off. He has started to put into practice what he has been learning in books and property seminars. He was after capital growth and good rent, by buying below market value, during an economic or property market slowdown and in good locations.
Paul bought these two properties at 90% and 95% LVR

respectively. He has set up a $100,000 line of credit linked to his house to help pay for the establishment cost and deposit on these two properties. He paid about $41,200 in property stamp duties, bank fees, mortgage insurance, and about $50,000 as deposits to acquire the two properties. He can claim most of the establishment costs over five years, except the property stamp duty which he can claim when he sells the property. His plan is to accumulate as many properties as possible, a total of 6-8 investments properties. His house is on a principal and interest repayment and linked to an offset account. He has spent a total of about $91,000 from his line of credit.

Table 1- his mortgage structure looks like this:

	PPOR- Home Joint name:	**Line of credit:**	**Property 1 His name:**	**Property 2 His name:**
Amount borrowed:	$160,000: ($80,000 for land & $120,000 building).	$100,000. -Drew or used about $91,000 to acquire these two properties. -Buffer or	$306,000.	$304,000.

		leftover $9,000.		
Bought for:	$200,000.		$340,000.	$320,000.
Valued at:	$400,000.		$420,000.	$380,000.
Deposit: Year acquired:	$40,000. Built in late 1999.		$34,000. Early 2001.	$16,000. Late 2001.
LVR:	80%		90%.	95%.
Stamp duty	$5,000 on the land.	None.	$10,500.	$10,000
Mortgage insurance	None.	None.	@$6,500.	@$6,000.
Other costs:	$2,000.	$700.	$4,000.	$4,200.
Equity in 2001.	Mortgage: $185,000.		$114,000.	$76,000.

	Equity: $215,000.			

Let's examine his situation now: his home was valued at $400,000, with a mortgage of $185,000. The equity was $215,000. Prior to buying their first property investment, Paul set up a line of credit of $100,000.

His first investment property in 2001:

It was valued at $420,000 and has a mortgage/debt of $306,000. The LVR was 90% and his equity was $114,000.

Property 2- investment 2001:

The property was valued at $380,000, with a mortgage of $304,000. The LVR was 95% and his equity was $76,000.

In 2005, the property is booming. Let's see the capital growth Paul has achieved on the three properties.

PPOR- Home :

Property valued at: $500,000. Debt: $185,000, plus $80,000 in the line of credit. Equity: $315,000. Capital growth of $100,000 or about 20% in 4 years.

Property investment 1:

Valued at: $500,000. Debt: $306,000.Your equity: $194,000. Capital growth of $80,000 or about 20% in 4 years.

Property investment 2:

Valued at: $450,000. Debt: $304,000. Your equity: $146,000. Capital growth of $70,000 or 20%. This is the magic of capital growth.

Table 1- his mortgage structure in 2005:

	PPOR- Home Joint name	**Line of credit:**	**Property 1: His name**	**Property 2: His name**
Debt:	$185,000 Line of credit: 150,000. **$315,000.**	$100,000 -Used up about $90,000. **May have increased this by another $50,000 to create a 'buffer.'**	$306,000	$304,000
Property valued:	$500,000		$500,000	$450,000
LVR currently:	63%		61%	67%
Equity:	$185,000		$194,000	$146,000

Capital growth in 4 years.	**$100,000 20%.**		**$80,000 @20%.**	**$70,000 @20%.**

Investor's tip:
Capital growth is the 'icing on the cake' as it is the money you make on your investment even when you're sleeping. This means that the higher the growth, the higher the equity available to draw on for further investments.

Diagram 1: his total equities from capital growth:

	PPOR (home)	**Property 1:**	**Property 2:**
Debts:	**$315,000**	**$306,000**	**$304,000**
Property value:	**$500,000**	**$500,000**	**$450,000**
New equity:	**$100,000**	**$80,000**	**$70,000**

Total equity:	**$185,000**	**$194,000**	**$146,000**

Total equity is: $525,000. This is the capital growth on the three properties in four years.

Let's see my capital growth in 4 years on my three properties.
My situation now– PPOR (Home) in 2010.

Property valued at: $400,000. Debt: $250,000. Equity: $150,000. I set up a line of credit of 35,000 in early 2007. I then increased this line of credit by another $80,000 in 2008. I paid $1,600 in lender's mortgage insurance and $1,000 in bank and other fees for this top up in 2008.

Property investment 1- Caversham:

Property valued at $360,000. Mortgage of $290,000. My equity of $70,000. Capital growth of $70,000 or about 20% in 4 years.

Property investment 2- The Vines:

Property valued at $400,000. Mortgage of $318,000. My equity of $82,000. Capital growth of $82,000 or about 20% in 4 years.

Capital growth and increasing rental income.

As my rental income have almost caught-up with interest repayment by cleverly fixing it, I will soon be in a position to afford the two new properties, depending on how easy it is to obtain finance, and bank's required LVR on new investments. I plan to acquire one to two property in 2010, and another one to two property in 2011.These new properties must cost around $300,000-$320,000 to be profitable and affordable and rented for about $320+ per week. I will then build two new properties in 2012-2013. Then my portfolio will be complete with about 6-8 property investments.

Chapter 2-

How to increase your cash flow to make money in real estate?

Financial tips to increase your cash flow to start you on the road to financial freedom fast: executive rental, student's accommodation and home-stay.

You can start on the road to financial freedom by:

- Saving for a deposit while at the same time establishing a saving history to be able to borrow money.

- Avoiding large personal debt.
- Working extra hours or a second job to pay for another property investment.
- Buying the house and rent the extra rooms to create cash flow for yourself.
- Renting each room individually to university students.
- 'Home-stay' to short-term overseas students. This income is tax free.
- Using your business to invest in property. Having a small business can be a good way to leverage into property investment.

Other ways to increase your cash: home-stay, write a book, good education and executive rental:

A- Rent your spare rooms and home-stay:

Many people with extra rooms can rent them out to overseas student, especially if your property is close to the city, educational institutions and public transport. If you live in Western Australia for example, there are many students from overseas who come to study at the major university institutions. There are companies which specialise in 'home-stay,' whereby overseas students 14 years+ who come to study English are invited to stay with a family. Get in contact with universities to see if you qualify to host these students in your home. You can get around $240 per week for each student. Those students stay for a short time, between 4 weeks to 3 months. All you have to do is cook for them and show them where to catch public transport. At first you may have to drop and pick them up until they familiarise themselves to the place. Then it's basically easy money that can go towards paying off your home loan or to pay off the short-fall on your property investment.

B- Write a book:

Why not write a book about your property adventure, your success and failure. This is a good way to educate people who are scared of investing. I wrote this book to help other people like myself. I want to make a contribution to society by educating people about property investing. I hope that those who buy the book, finds it valuable and informative. I'm not a guru in property investing. I'm not a self-made millionaire. But what I want to do is to tell my story to the world. I haven't fully achieved my goal but I'm on the road to achieving this within ten years. My life is easier and better than it was before 2005. I'm a property owner with property investments on top of that. You can see where property investment has taken me since 2005.

C- Good education:

I've learnt a lot learnt from writing these two books as I had to think and write down all the things that I'm doing and have done in property investing. I've also included all the mistakes that I've made. It is good to learn from other's mistakes because this is the only way you can learn and become a successful property investor.

D- Executive rental:

If you have a nice two to three bedrooms and two bathrooms fully furnished but stylish apartments in the inner city or close to the city centre, you can market it as an executive rental. These tenants are usually on a short-term contract working for large corporations.

Their employer/company pays for their accommodation. Sometimes properties close to large industrial areas are sought after by large companies for their expatriate specialist staff. Providing that the tenants and the company like your property, they are likely to rent it for their workers at a premium rent. Your property must be of high quality, easy to maintain and have good security. The property must be close to good schools and major specialist businesses. Executive renters like to live close to their work and close to the CBD and want good quality and well-maintained properties. They expect quality services such pay TV, Internet connection, security gates, intercom, DVDs or a car for the high rent they're paying.

How to find them?

Go online and look for large corporations looking for property to rent. Look in the Yellow Pages for large corporations, relocation consultants /services or by approaching them yourself. You can market your property online through holiday accommodation websites. Also, contact real estate and travel agents for their advice. You will pay a small fee for their services.

Advantages of executive rental:

- Higher rental income: the rent is normally about $1,000 to $2,500 per week for apartment rooms with water views and about $1,000 to $5,000 for family homes.
- Once executive renters find a place they like, they generally stay longer.
- You get to use the property when it is not being rented. Some renters are short term such as the weekends and others are a bit longer, 1-3 years lease.

Part 6-
Managing property and preparing for tax return.

Chapter 1.

Property management for first time property investors.

Understanding property management, lease agreement and landlord obligation and preparing for tax return.

Why it is important to use a good property manager to manage your property?

A good property manager should do the following for you:

- They manage and look for suitable tenants for your property.

- Advertise the property, collect rent and deposit the proceeds in your bank account.
- Arrange for property maintenance, do quarterly property inspections and provide you with a written property condition report and photos.
- Provide you with a monthly/fortnightly rental statement and with an annual rental statement to be used for your tax return.
- Deal with any issues that may arise on the property and smooth out transition from one tenant to another.

For a tax deductible fee of between 10-12% of the rental income, my property managers take total care of my investment property and provide the additional services:

- Ensure that the new tenant sign a lease agreement which stipulate in writing all the landlords and tenants obligations and rights.
- Let the tenants know if there would be rent increased/reviewed.
- States clearly to tenants what can and can't be done on the property.
- Ensure that tenants maintain the property in its original condition.
- They collect a bond and rent on time. They can take the necessary steps to rectify any unpaid rent.

Why do we need a property condition report and a lease agreement signed at the start of the lease?

Lease agreement is designed to prevent misunderstanding and

disagreement between renters and landlords. Many landlords who manage their property themselves, like to tell their tenants things orally rather than in writing. This should be avoided. Written lease agreement will minimise disputes with tenants. You will have the proof to show the tenants that this was agreed and signed off at the lease agreement.

When to increase rent?

When deciding to increase rent to take advantage of property boom and cope with interest rate rises, landlords need to consider:

- The existing rent and when was the last rent increase.
- The vacancy rate in the vicinity and the rent of similar properties.
- The time of the year and the property cycle-boom or downswing.
- The possibility of a good tenant vacating, the cost of re-advertising for a new tenant and how good and reliable is the existing tenant.

While rent increases is vital, it is profitable to keep a property rented at all times. There is a limit on what an owner can charge and a process for rent increases. Landlords cannot increase rent during a fixed-term lease, unless the contract stipulates that. When signing for a new tenant, landlords cannot ask for more than two weeks rent in advance plus bond. Tenants have the right to challenge sudden and excessive rent increases in the Local Court. Rents can be increased with each new and renewed contract, but only every six months. Ask for a copy of the annual rental statement from your property managing agent. This will make it easier to do your tax return.

Investor's tip:

In cases where there is no written agreement, landlords can increase rent only after giving two month's notice to the tenants before the lease expires.

Preparing for tax return.

You need to keep:

1. The interest paid and loan statements. Ask your bank for this.
2. All loan documents.
3. All your receipts of accommodation, and the logbook or record of travel to inspect the property.
4. An annual property statement report for all of your rented property. Ask your real estate manager for one.
5. Your depreciation schedule.

What deductions can you legally claim?

The net rental/property loss is the negative gearing that can be fully claimed from your taxes.

These are items you can claim each year:

- Interest repayment, insurance, land tax, bank fees, property management fees, stationery, telephone and postage.
- Personal income protection, landlord and building insurance and borrowing expenses such as valuation, mortgage stamp duty (not land stamp duty), loan establishment, title search and lender's mortgage insurance fees.
- Travel expenses– use a log book. Buy one at post offices or news-agencies.

- Phone and electricity bills at a rate of 20% each year.
- Depreciating fittings and fixtures can be claimed over the life of the items. Building over 40 years (new property).
- Maintenance expenses such as gardening/lawn mowing, pest control fees and repairs.

Investor's tip:
Establishment expenses can be claimed when the property is sold: landscaping and renovation expenses, stamp duty and settlement agent fees. These items are added to the cost of the property for reducing or calculating capital gains tax (CGT).

Part 7- Understanding the tax benefits of property investing and the importance of property valuation.

Chapter 1.
How to legally reduce your tax and using it to create wealth for yourself?

Maximising tax deductions: don't overpay income tax.

This can be achieved by:

- Claiming all deductions and expenses.
- Using six months lease and reviewing rent every six months.
- Buying during slump and selling during booms and reinvest the profits. Buy now when everyone is selling.
- Buying property below market value. Buy the cheapest property in the best suburb.

- Adding value and then leverage: you can achieve capital growth by renovating a property. Sometimes all that's needed is a small TLC such as new carpet and tiling, painting, a new kitchen, front and backyard improvement. You need to avoid extensive improvements as this can blow your budget and destroy the extra equity that you're trying to achieve.

Adding value can be beneficial in two ways:

- Capital gains or increase value which can be used as a deposit for another property.
- Increased cash flow as a renovated property will attract tenants prepared to pay higher rent.

Distinguishing between tax deductible and non-tax deductible deductions on rental properties:

You need to know what the tax office defines as repair compared to improvement. Repair is generally replacing a worn out item such as fixtures and fittings while property improvements is replacing a whole unit such as a new fence, a new kitchen, flooring, and repainting the whole house before tenants move in. Ask the tax office or your accountant for advice before you undertake any property improvements or renovations. As a property investor, it is important to claim everything that are legally claimable and avoiding costly mistakes when dealing with the ATO.

Some common mistakes property investors can make each tax year include:

- Claiming property improvements as repairs.

- Overstating rental deductions by not correctly apportioning borrowings between business and private use.
- Claiming deductions for the whole year when the property was only rented for only part of the year.

Some improvements which can mistakenly claimed as repairs are:

- Replacing the whole item: a new fence or kitchen
- Re-plastering, re-flooring or re-tiling a property.
- Repainting a whole house that had worn out paint when it was bought.
- Building an extra room, garage; alterations such as adding or removing an internal wall.
- Adding a deck, carport or driveway will be classed as capital works.

Avoid costly mistakes if you want to be a successful property investor.

Awareness of what is considered deductions on rental properties is vital. Avoid making mistakes when dealing with the tax office. Avoid overstating rental deductions as the tax office will eventually find out, costing you substantially. Make sure that you don't claim property improvements as repairs. Keep proper record and use a competent and registered accountant to do your tax return. Only claim deductions for part of the year, if it had been rented for that long.

Tax tips for property investors:

To ensure you get the most from your investments, you need to know what the taxation office defines as repairs and improvements.

Repair is generally replacing a worn out or damage items which are part of the fixtures and fittings such as the blinds, damage floors and fence.

1. When you buy a property with the intention of renting it, the cost of repairing or improving to make the property rent-able is part of the cost of its acquisition, not an initial repair and can be claimed when you sell the property.
2. You're entitled to claim your travel expenses to inspect the property, do repair on the property or collect rent. Keep a log book of the date and kilometres travelled. You can claim about 70 cents a kilometre. There is a limit of 5000 kilometres for each property owner. A total of 10,000 kilometres for both spouses and owners using the same car. You can claim expenses as long as the main purpose of the trip is to inspect the properties. If you stay overnight in a hotel, you can claim that expense too. If you travel to inspect your property and then stay on for a few more days, you have to apportion the private from business use. Normally, you can claim a maximum of two days of travel and accommodation expenses.
3. Consider pre-paying interest on the rental property up to 12 months in advance and get a tax deduction in the year it is paid. But this only work when the properties are positively geared.
4. Even if the investment property has been emptied due to renovation or vacant in tough times, you are still entitled to full deductions.
5. If you jointly own a property with your partner and she/he is not working, her or his deductions may be wasted. Avoid this by planning ahead. If your wife is going to be home and looking after

the kids, it may be wise to put the property in the name of the person who will be working at all times.

Property depreciation benefits:

Property depreciation schedule is a report that allows you to claim deductions for decline in value on a building used for earning an income. It is a vital part of property deduction entitlements, whether your property is cash flow positively or negatively geared. Claiming this deduction can mean saving thousands of dollars each year. There are provisions in the tax laws that allow you to claim up to four years of missed depreciations. Check with your tax agent or accountant. **The report contains two parts:**

A- Depreciating building:

You can claim the cost of the building as a depreciating asset. With a rate of 2.5% and 4% (on some property) annually, you can claim thousands of dollars over 40 years, if you live in Australia.

B- Depreciating fittings and fixtures:

These items can be claimed usually over five years and longer based on their life. Items such as hot water systems, carpets, blinds and air-conditioning will receive a tax deduction. All items connected to the building have a life, and a depreciating value. Let's have a look at the depreciation schedule for my property investment below. The building cost $130,000. I spent about $15,000 on installing the flooring, air-conditioning, window blinds, the backyard paving and front lawn.

Claiming all your legal tax deductions will help you to:

- Avoid paying more tax than you should.
- Use the extra cash to pay off non-deductible debt such as

your house (PPOR).

- Reduce property expenses and reduce pressure on your finances.

There are four main groups of deductions.

A- Immediate deductions claim annually:

These items can be claimed immediately each year as part of your property expenses. It includes things such as shire and water rates, interest repayments, property maintenance and insurance, travel and accommodation.

B- Depreciating building, fittings and fixtures:

Items which are part of the property such as depreciating buildings, fittings and fixtures which can be claimed each year over 40 years (new property).

C- Deductions claim over 5 years:

Borrowing expenses can be claimed over five years if they are more than $300. Things such as valuation fees, mortgage stamp duty, loan establishment fees, title search fees, land tax and lender's mortgage insurance fees. Also, you can claim tax deductions for depreciating business equipment at a rate of 20% annually. **Things such as:**

- Land-line and mobile phone, computers, laptop, printers and faxes.
- Electricity bill.

D- Deductions you can claim when you sell the asset:

Establishment expenses and all borrowing costs are rounded up and closed when the property is sold. Expenses, like landscaping/renovations, stamp duty to state government and settlement agent fees. These items are deducted from the capital gains when you sell the property.

Incomes which your property losses can be claimed against include:

- Income from your wage/salary, from business, share portfolio and other positive rental income.

The benefits of having a depreciation schedule.

Table 1- property without a depreciation schedule:

Yearly income:	**$100,000**
Tax rate @30% and tax paid:	**$30,000**
Rental income:	**$16,640**
Depreciation deductions:	**0**
Total expenses	**$26,647**
Rental loss	**$10,007**
Taxable income:	**$89,993**
Tax saving:	**@$3,500.**

Tax saving: @$3,500.

Table 2- property with a depreciation schedule:

Yearly income:	$100,000
Tax rate @30% and tax paid:	$30,000
Rental income:	$16,640
Total property expenses:	$26,467
Depreciation deductions:	$5,000
Total expenses	$31,467
Rental loss	$16,460
Taxable income:	$83,540
Tax saving:	@$5,000.

That's an extra $1,500 saving by having a depreciation schedule. Multiply this by the number of investment properties you have, that's more money in your pocket.

The diagram is a depreciation benefits of my property at The vines, in Western Australia.

It cost me $318,000 to build. The land cost $175,000 and the building, fittings and fixtures cost about $143,000. As you can see from the two diagrams below, I can claim all this $143,000 as tax deductions over 40 years (new property), leaving only the land which will increase in value over time.

Depreciation summary of the property at The Vines:

Plant (fittings and fixtures:	**$14,823**
Capital works allowances (building)	**$128,011**
A total of:	**$142,834**

1.0 SUMMARY OF ENTITLEMENTS

	SUMMARY OF CLAIM BY USING DIMINISHING VALUE METHOD				OR	SUMMARY OF CLAIM BY USING PRIME COST METHOD		
	Depreciation on Plant	Low Value Pooling	Capital Allowances	Yearly Total		Depreciation on Plant	Capital Allowances	Yearly Total
Financial Year	$	$	$	$		$	$	$
7/7/2006 - 2007	1,963 +	273 +	3,288 =	5,524	or	1,717 +	3,288 =	5,005
2007 - 2008	1,131 +	444 +	3,343 =	4,918		1,066 +	3,343 =	4,409
2008 - 2009	971 +	277 +	3,343 =	4,591		1,066 +	3,343 =	4,409
2009 - 2010	833 +	173 +	3,343 =	4,349		1,066 +	3,343 =	4,409
2010 - 2011	715 +	289 +	3,343 =	4,347		1,066 +	3,343 =	4,409
2011 - 2012	614 +	0 +	3,343 =	3,957		952 +	3,343 =	4,295
2012 - 2013	527 +	0 +	3,343 =	3,870		950 +	3,343 =	4,293
2013 - 2014	453 +	0 +	3,343 =	3,796		950 +	3,343 =	4,293
2014 - 2015	389 +	0 +	3,343 =	3,732		950 +	3,343 =	4,293
2015 - 2016	334 +	0 +	3,343 =	3,677		950 +	3,343 =	4,293
2016 - 2017	287 +	0 +	3,343 =	3,630		358 +	3,343 =	3,701
2017 - 2018	247 +	0 +	3,343 =	3,590		348 +	3,343 =	3,691
2018 - 2019	212 +	0 +	3,343 =	3,555		7 +	3,343 =	3,350
2019 - 2020	182 +	0 +	3,343 =	3,525		0 +	3,343 =	3,343
2020 - 2021	157 +	0 +	3,343 =	3,500		0 +	3,343 =	3,343
2021 - 2022	135 +	0 +	3,343 =	3,478		0 +	3,343 =	3,343
2022 - 2023	116 +	0 +	3,343 =	3,459		0 +	3,343 =	3,343
2023 - 2024	100 +	0 +	3,343 =	3,443		0 +	3,343 =	3,343
2024 - 2025	86 +	0 +	3,343 =	3,429		0 +	3,343 =	3,343
2025 - 2026	74 +	0 +	3,343 =	3,417		0 +	3,343 =	3,343
2026 - 2027	64 +	0 +	3,343 =	3,407		0 +	3,343 =	3,343
2027 - 2028	55 +	0 +	3,343 =	3,398		0 +	3,343 =	3,343
2028 - 2029	47 +	0 +	3,343 =	3,390		0 +	3,343 =	3,343
2029 - 2030	41 +	0 +	3,343 =	3,384		0 +	3,343 =	3,343
2030 - 2031	35 +	0 +	3,343 =	3,378		0 +	3,343 =	3,343
2031 - 2032	30 +	0 +	3,343 =	3,373		0 +	3,343 =	3,343
2032 - 2033	26 +	0 +	3,343 =	3,369		0 +	3,343 =	3,343
2033 - 2034	22 +	0 +	3,343 =	3,365		0 +	3,343 =	3,343
2034 - 2035	19 +	0 +	3,343 =	3,362		0 +	3,343 =	3,343
2035 - 2036	17 +	0 +	3,343 =	3,360		0 +	3,343 =	3,343
2036 - 2037	14 +	0 +	3,343 =	3,357		0 +	3,343 =	3,343
2037 - 2038	12 +	0 +	3,343 =	3,355		0 +	3,343 =	3,343
2038 - 2039	11 +	0 +	3,343 =	3,354		0 +	3,343 =	3,343
2039 - 2040	9 +	0 +	3,343 =	3,352		0 +	3,343 =	3,343
2040 - 2041	8 +	0 +	3,343 =	3,351		0 +	3,343 =	3,343
2041 - 2042	7 +	0 +	3,343 =	3,350		0 +	3,343 =	3,343
2042 - 2043	6 +	0 +	3,343 =	3,349		0 +	3,343 =	3,343
2043 - 2044	5 +	0 +	3,343 =	3,348		0 +	3,343 =	3,343
2044 - 2045	4 +	0 +	3,343 =	3,347		0 +	3,343 =	3,343
2045 - 2046	29 +	0 +	2,991 =	3,020		0 +	2,991 =	2,991
Total	**$9,988 +**	**$1,456 +**	**$133,313 =**	**$144,757**		**$11,444 +**	**$133,313 =**	**$144,757**

Investor's tip:
Remember you cannot claim the land as a depreciation deduction as land appreciates while building depreciates each year. New properties will receive full depreciation benefits.

Tax variation- you don't have to wait until June 30 to access the tax benefit.

It is possible to claim your tax deductions every time you get paid. This means you don't have to wait until the end of financial year to claim the deductions. This can be arranged by you filling out a tax variation form whereby when you estimate your expenses or losses and claim your tax deductions immediately. It will take about six weeks for it to be approved. Visit www.ato.gov.au and download a tax variation form. I was able to reduce my taxes from $582 to $134 each fortnight last year, giving me an extra $448 to cover the shortfall on my investment. A lot of property investors are forced to sell their investment property due to cash shortfall and most could have kept their property if they knew about the tax variation law.

Below is an example of a tax variation. It is for this financial year (2009-2010). In this example, my tax payment has been reduced from $650 to $350, giving me an extra $300 each fortnight.

Diagram- here is an example of how the tax variation:

Locked Bag 1515 Upper Mt Gravatt QLD 4122

Mr Wilnes A Radegonde

Telephone: 1300 360 221
Facsimile: (07) 3213 3188

Email: ITWvariation@ato.gov.a

Our reference: ITWV/35551

24 July 2009

Dear Mr Radegonde

Your withholding variation application

For your information

Thank you for lodging your application for the 2010 financial year. We have varied the withholding rate to be applied to the gross payments listed below to 12% per payment.

Gross payments: salary and wages

A separate notice has been sent to your payer/s, advising them of the variation to the amount withheld.

This variation applies from the next available payment until 30 June 2010. Normal withholding rates will apply from 1 July 2010 unless you apply and receive approval for a new variation before that date. Please apply for this renewal at least six weeks prior to 30 June 2010 if you want a variation to continue after this date.

Chapter 2- Maximising tax deductions- structuring property ownership correctly.

It is important that you understand the tax system in the country where you live. Buying a property is only part of the game. You need to set up the right structure. That's why you need to plan ahead with your partner for the future. If it is a negatively geared property, it might be best to have the property in the name of the highest income earner. The person with the highest income will pay more taxes and get the most deductions and highest tax return.

If the property is in the name of the lowest income earner, that person will receive the lowest deduction. If it is positively geared then it might be best to place it in the name of the lowest income earner to reduce taxation liabilities. If you plan to sell one property soon, it is best to have the property in the name of the lowest income earner. But you also need to plan for long-term change in your circumstances. Putting the property in the wrong name will cost you thousands of dollars each year in loss of tax deductions or tax liability. So, plan carefully before you buy. The name on the property title/deed is the person who owns the property for taxation purposes.

It might be best to put the property losing the smallest amount of money or returning positive income in the name of the lowest income earner to reduce tax liability. But you also need to decide which property is likely to be cash flow positive the fastest? Who is going to work less hours in the future? Is your wife is going to have a baby soon? Which property will you sell in the next few years to pay off your home (PPOR)? These things are important considerations when buying properties and registering ownership. The person on the highest tax rate pays more tax on any positive income. If you want to change the property ownership later, it will cost you thousands of dollars in stamp duty, settlement agent fees, capital gains tax and other transfer costs at current market value. This could well destroy all the tax benefits you have gained through the change of ownership.

Let's have a look at the property establishment cost involved in buying a $260,000 property and what you have to pay again if you change your mind later.

This could include:

- $10,000+ in stamp duty.
- Another- $1,193+ in costs of disbursements as shown in the example.
- Legal fees.
- Other fees.

Importance of putting the property ownership in the right name for maximum tax deductions.

Table 1- the property with 100% ownership:

Yearly income:	$150,000

Tax paid @45%	$67,500
Rental income	$10,000
Total property expenses/deductions	$17,500
Rental loss:	$7,500
Tax saving:/refund:	@$3,375.

Total saving: $3,375. The couple save $3,375 by having the property in the name of the highest income earner.

Table 2- the $300,000 property in joint names:

	Husband	Wife
Yearly income:	$100,000	0
Tax paid @45%	$67,500	0
Rental income	$5,000	$5,000
Total property expenses/deductions	$8,750	$8,750
Rental loss:	$3,750	$3,750

Tax saving:/refund:	@$1,687.	0.

Total saving: $1,687. Her tax deductions are wasted as she has no income to claim this loss against. This is a loss of $1,687 for the couple. This is the result of poor planning. It cost the couple thousands of dollars to change property ownership.

Investor's tip:

Plan ahead and put the property (properties) in the right name to maximise tax deductions and minimise tax liabilities. Income earning property should be in the name of the lowest income earner and property losing money in the name of the highest income earner.

Chapter 3-
Property valuation and its importance in property investing and wealth creation.

Valuation: how much is your property worth?

Property valuation is the act of trying to assess a property to determine it's value. It is an educated assessment of the characteristics of the property and the market conditions at the time of valuation. A valuation will help you to know the value of the property at the time and avoid paying too much. A real estate agent appraisal or estimation of the value of your property is not a bank approved 'valuation' that you can use to borrow money. Property valuation will help to determine if the timing is right for selling or whether it's best to wait.

Valuations are used by the bank when you apply for finance to buy a property or for revaluation after property improvements for equity release loans. The lender will usually have an independent valuation panel of approved valuers who carry out property valuation. Those valuers usually work for the bank but you can get them to carry out a valuation on a property before you buy. Normally, you cannot choose your valuer if you're applying for a loan with a lender as the valuer will be chosen by the lender and not by you.

Buying a property without a property valuation can be costly as cost doesn't always equal value. In a new property, the combined cost of the land and building sometimes are more than the property value. Many people spend too much on building cost. Sale price of a property sometimes doesn't determine its actual value. Many sellers put the price of their property above the market value hoping to make a big profit. A real estate agent appraisal or estimation of the value of your property is not a bank approved 'valuation' that you can use to borrow money. The market is constantly changing and a valuation must be no more than three months old for it to be relied on.

What influence can you have on the outcome of the valuation?

Ensure that the valuer physically inspected the property. If you can find any evidence of comparable sales present these to the valuer before the valuer submits his/her finding to the bank. You cannot influence the valuer as he/she tends to be very cautious and works for the bank. Valuers inspect the property and use computer and available sales evidence to make a final decision. They use sales data and the characteristics of the property to help them make an informed decision.

You can order an independent valuation yourself to find out the value of the property and compare to the bank's valuer. This will ensure that you don't pay too much and if possible bargain and buy below market value. Remember, equity is the sum or profits that you've made on your property over the years and it is important to keep it. Lower valuations can crippled your ability to grow your property.

What determines a property's value?

(a) The economic conditions.

(b) The size of the land and building.

(c) Good location of the property- close to the city centre, the ocean or the river.

(d) Quality of the fittings, fixtures and conditions inside the dwelling. Is it a new or old property?

(e) Security features such as garage, roller shutters and security grills on windows.

(f) Facilities in the property such as air-conditioning, alfresco or patio.

(g) Presentation of the inside and outside of the property.

(h) Does it have a good vehicle access? Is it on a busy street or road?

Why is property valuation important?

- Financial institutions use it to lend money to investors or property owners.
- It will determine if there is enough security/equity in the property to lend you the fund you require.
- It will determine if you will pay lender's mortgage insurance and how much.
- It gives an idea of the direction of the market. Is it booming or slowing down?

Placing a lower valuation on your property will cost you a lot in terms of higher lender's mortgage insurance to be paid or not be able to borrow all the fund you want.

Investor's tip:

Equity or LVR is calculated by using the debt amount divided by the property value. For example, if the debt on the property

is $360,000 and the property is valued at $500,000, the equity is calculated: $360,000 divide by $500,000= 0.72%.

Diagram 1- the importance of property valuation. His home (PPOR):

In 2006, the owner's house was valued at $400,000. The debt was $300,000 and the equity was $100,000. The LVR (lending valuation ratio) was 75%. The owner used his home to borrow money to invest in property.

Valued: $400,000
Equity: $100,000
Debt: $300,000

This means that the owner can borrow an extra 5% ($20,000) without paying any lender's mortgage insurance and without declaring his income if he has a business number (ABN). If he borrows up to 95% of the property value ($380,000 for an investment property), his lender's mortgage insurance fee will be about 2% of the total amount being borrowed or $7,000. The debt on his home has increased to $320,000 (5%).

Diagram 2- his new equity position:

Valued: $400,000

Equity: $80,000
Debt: $320,000

Diagram 3- the importance of property valuation:

In 2008, due to increased property value (rising prices), the property was valued at $600,000. The debt was still $320,000 as the owner has an interest only loan on the investment property to maximise tax deductions. The equity has now increased by $200,000.

Valued at: $600,000
Equity: $240,000
Debt: $320,000

This means that the owner can borrow up to 80% of the property value (an extra $160,000) without paying any lender's mortgage insurance. So, he goes ahead and borrow the $160,000 from the equity and buy/build 1-2 properties with this fund.

Diagram 4: his equity position:

Valued at: $600,000

Equity: $120,000
Debt: $480,000

Diagram 5- decreased in property value:

Valued at: $500,000
Equity: $20,000
Debt: $480,000

In 2010, due to the financial crisis, the property has decreased in value and was now worth at $500,000. The equity has decreased by $100,000. The LVR (lending valuation ratio) was now 96%. He cannot borrow any money on his home until it increases in value again. So, lower valuation has reduced his wealth and equity in his home.

Investor's tip:
It is a good idea to evaluate all your properties in your portfolio

every 1-2 years to ascertain if the properties are performing according to expectations and to borrow available equity for more investments or for increasing your buffer funds.

Part 8-
Asset protection.

Chapter 1.
How to protect assets from litigation and from repossession.

Protecting your assets from tenants, repossession and litigation.
Protecting your valuable and hard earned asset is the best part of investing. There is no point working hard and investing to accumulate assets only to lose your properties in a law suit and other reasons.

Borrowing money to serve as a buffer for asset protection.

1. An equity release line of credit.
Get a line of credit as soon as your property has increased in value. This will allow you to keep the asset and benefit in the long run. It is a small price to pay for financial freedom. Equity loan is a good way to borrow money to increase your buffer funds. This loan is very good as you don't have to increase your home loan balance directly. You just borrow the extra money in a separate line of credit.

Advantages of a buffer fund borrowed as home improvements:

- The interest rates you pay is the same as a home loan interest rates.
- You can pay interest only and claim all the interests on your

income tax paid.

- You pay interest only on the amount you've drawn down.
- It helps you to sleep at night, knowing that you have cash handy in case you need it.

For example, in 2008, I borrowed $80,000 on my investment property by increasing my line of credit. The money was borrowed as property improvement. I used the fund to install an air-conditioning unit and complete the backyard paving on the property. I had $70,000 leftover which I used to increase my buffer fund.

Diagram- using a line of credit as an asset protection- buffer

fund

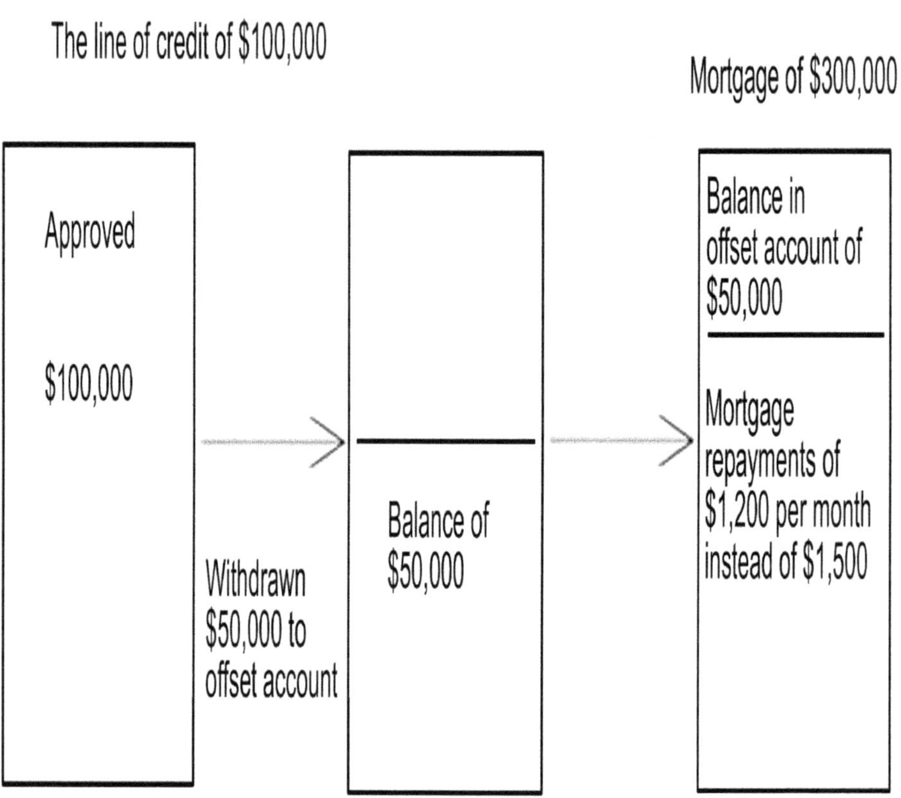

You have $100,000 buffer fund to protect your property and at the same time as it is linked to an offset account, it is saving you interest on that loan.

2. Have an income or business protection insurance:
Make sure you get an income, mortgage or business protection insurance straight away. This will give you peace of mind. It's like a life jacket. My income protection insurance is with a company called "Insurance Line." It protects against loss of income from events such as job loss or an accident. This is a must for property investors. This insurance will provide me with an income of ($4,600) or 75% of my current income for up to two years, while I recover or look for a new job. It cost me about $75 per month. A two months waiting period generally applies to claims.
3. Landlord protection, building and content insurance:
As a landlord, it is important to keep your rented property in good condition and that you're protected against all kinds of disasters and problems such as malicious damage by tenants and rent default. Unless you're insured, you can be out of pocket by thousands of dollars. My landlord, content and building insurance are with Westpac General Insurer and CGU Insurance. It is estimated that 1/3 of property investors don't have landlord insurance. For about $2 a day, you can protect your property for up to $20 million in public liability insurance in case you're sued by your tenants and their guests for accidents while staying in your property.
It is important that you keep your insurance up-to date by regularly increasing the payout amount. You should review your insurance every 6-12 months to keep pace with inflation. For example, building cost can go up by 10-20% each year. So, unless you've updated your insurance, you can be under-insured by 10-20% each year.

4. Life insurance:

This generally provides a lump sum payment to your family in the event of death or terminal illness.

5. A good managing agent:

Choose an agent that will do a routine 3 months property inspection and provide you with a written report and photos of the property. My property at Caversham is managed by Allied Residential marketers in Western Australia. Visit: www:alliedresidentialmarketers.com or by calling 08-93230788. My property at "The vines" in Western Australia is managed by The Vines Real Estate. Visit: www.thevinesrealestate.com for a good property manager.

6. Short-term loan:

Avoid waiting for the bailiff to knock on your door. If you have to borrow a loan from a private lending institution to keep the property until you sell, then do it. A company called "Financial express" is an example of a short-term funding institution. There are many short-term lenders out there that provide short-term loans of 3-12 months. You can refinance the loan every 3 months.

Most short term lenders will lend you between $5,000 to $50,000 and charge between 25% in interest and fees. A $20,000 loan for three months will cost you about $5,000 in interest and fees. So, if you find yourself in a difficult situation, running out of cash or a loss of job and you have to sell, then by all means give these lenders a go.

7. Personal loan:

It is not a bad idea to get a personal loan to keep your head above water. Remember, this is an emergency, if you desperately need it. This might help you avoid having to sell your property. A $20,000 personal loan for example can be a lifeline in times of financial hardship. When your situation improves, refinance the personal loan into your house (PPOR) to reduce your repayment.

8. Refinance to a cheaper loan or to get additional cash reserve:
You should look at refinancing your mortgage. Switch to a new lender for a better deal. Any money saved will help to reduce your property losses and holding cost.

9. Borrowing in good times in preparation for bad times:
It is a wise investment strategy to always have extra cash handy. You must always be prepared for bad things to happen. Always borrow in good times, even if you don't need the money now. Leave it in a line of credit or offset account just in case you need it later.

10. Good planning:
Think ahead and avoid the kind of situation where you suddenly realise that you don't have enough money, or your wife is pregnant and you need extra cash. You should not tell the bank that only one of you is now working, and you want to borrow some money. They will probably refuse you. Lending institutions are in the business of making money and like to look after their own interests. It is silly to see people losing their home to the bank when they still have plenty of equity in it. The bank will fire-sale on your assets and this will prevent you from borrowing money and owning another property for at least 5 years. Banks are not your friend. So keep

your personal problems to yourself. They may help you in hard times (recession) for a maximum of 6 months of capitalisation of loan repayments (no loan repayments to be made).

11. Keep a clean credit file at all times:

Avoid defaulting on any loans or bills at all costs. A clean credit file means that you are a valuable customer and in a crisis, they will lend you the cash you desperately need.

12. Get a credit card:

Get a credit card if you're cash poor to help you pay bills until your situation improves. If you find that after paying off the mortgage, you have little cash left to put food on the table and pay bills, a credit card can help you temporarily. Get one with a $10,000 limit which has a good rate and 55 days interest free. Refinance the balance to a new bank which has a 0% transfer for 6 months in one year's time, if you haven't paid it off. This way you can still use your pay-cheque to maintain your loan repayments.

13 . Get a tax variation:

Tax variation-apply for a tax variation now if you have property investments and you're struggling financially. This will ease your financial pressure.

14. A family/unit trust:

For this, you need to consult an accountant expert in this field to help you set one up. Rich people tend to use family trust to pass on their assets to their children and pay less tax. People in high risk job or business people with a lot of debt, might use one to protect their assets from being lost in a lawsuit or bankruptcy.

Disadvantages:

- The longer you wait to do that, the more will be the transfer fees for stamp duty, capital gains and legal fees as these will be calculated on the capital growth of the property.
- You might not be able to claim any negative gearing benefits when the property is in a family trust.
- The potential tax benefits of the trust must outweigh the property costs of the property for it to be profitable.
- There is ongoing and annual trust costs.
- If you decide to set one up, you will pay a one off solicitor's fee of around $500-$2,000.
- If you don't distribute all the incomes from the trustee and it accumulates, that income will be taxed at the highest marginal tax rate.
- A trust might not protect the assets effectively if there is a divorce unless both partners have agreed (pre-nup arrangement) before the relationship breakdown.
- Place investment properties and not your PPOR in the trust as you might lose your Capital Gains Tax Exemption which applies to your house.
- The trust is now to be in control of your assets and not you.
- What if your circumstances changes and you want control of your assets?
- If your spouses and children are on higher incomes, the tax advantages may not work well.

Advantages:

- It will work better if your properties are cash flow positive or becoming cash flow positive.
- Might work well if you are in a high risk job such as a doctor. You will still need to get indemnity insurance for added protection.
- Usually effective protection from creditors after 5 years. The trust can't be sued to recover personal losses as you don't own the assets.
- There is asset protection, but most of your assets will be covered by public liability insurance anyway.
- Tax saving and income distribution. The trust can distribute positive rental income and capital gains among different family members, rather than leaving all in the name of the highest income earner and thereby reducing the tax bill.
- Keep assets in the family and pass onto the next generation.
- It might reduce your land tax bill depending on which state or country you live and their laws. Check this out with your accountant.
- If the assets are sold and the beneficiaries are on a lower income, they will pay less capital gains tax (CGT).

Part 9-
Planning to retire early and having an exit Strategy.

Chapter 1.
Having an exit strategy and understanding how capital gains tax works.

As a property investor it is important to have an exit strategy in case you need to sell a property if your circumstances change such as divorce, loss of job, low capital growth and or the economy slows down and you cannot get decent rent. You need to decide when it's time to sell, especially if you've over-commit yourself and struggling. It is important not to default and tarnish your credit rating. If the property has failed to deliver on your expectations and it is costing you the earth, then it is time to sell. **These are simple tips when selling your investment property:**

- Use a local agent as they are more knowledgeable than non-local agents. Advertise as much as possible in newspapers and on-line but avoid over-spending.
- Price the property correctly and avoid over-pricing it.
- Select an agent who will provide you with frequent update and feedback.
- Make sure that the street is clean, fresh, and the front garden

is appealing as first impression is important.

- Fixed any cracks in the building. The room must be bright in terms of having natural light penetrate the house. Add a couple of large mirrors to make the rooms look bigger.
- Tidied up the place and remove unnecessary furniture.

Calculating capital gains tax (CGT):

You can make or lose money on a property at the time of sale. If you've had the asset for more than 12 months, you are entitled to a bonus 50% discount on the capital gains. If you made a net capital gain, you will pay tax on this profit. Capital gains tax is very important for property investors. Capital gains tax is usually excluded from the family home. In Australia, if you buy a house live in it and then rent it out and later sell it, you're exempted from CGT if the sale falls within 6 years of owning that property. But this only works if you don't have another property that you're claiming as your PPOR.

This is an example of capital gain tax of a property costing $290,000:

Ownership:

50% Wilnes 50% Yamin

Sale price ($390,000). **Gross capital gain before tax: $79,000**
Mortgage: $285,000.
Deposit: $11,000

Establishment costs: $15,000
Property loses after tax over the 2 years: 2006-2007-@$8,000 last year and $20,000 this year.
Inflation over the 2 years @2% annually, say @$5,000
Discount of 50% on gross capital gain: $39,000
Gross capital gains to be taxed: @$39,000
Our real gain/profit was about: $40,000.

Our net capital gain for taxation purposes was about $19,000. But our real gain was about $40,000.

1. Net capital gains for tax purposes: $9,500 for my wife and $9,500 for me. My wife was a low income earner with a gross income of $20,000. Her taxable income was now $29,500. She paid very little tax on this capital gains.
1. As for me, I paid about $2,000 in tax on that $9,500.
2. To fully calculate the real capital gains/profits, you need to add inflation cost for the two years you've had the property.
3. The previous year’s losses after tax on the property.

This will be more of an accurate picture of your capital gains and profits from the property. So, our total profits were about $40,000.

Important note:

If you've owned the property for more than one year, you get 50% discount on the $100,000 gross capital gains. This means you pay tax on $50,000 but only after deducting any property loss for this year. If your net capital gain is $30,000 and you're on a tax rate of 30%, the capital gains tax will be: $30,000 X 30%=$9,000. If your tax rate is 45%, the capital gains tax will be $30,000 X 45%=13,500. If you're on a lower tax of 10%, the capital gains tax will be 30,000 X 10%=$3,000. So, your tax rate affects your tax liability. The lower income earners pays less CGT than a higher income earner. Alternatively, you can move into this investment and sell it within a year as your PPOR and pay no tax. Use all the proceeds to pay off the house you intend to live in as your PPOR.

What records to keep?

- Records of real estate sale agent, settlement agent's, accounting and advertising fees.
- Insurance fees, shire, water rates and land tax bills.
- Evidence of sale of property and how much you sold it for.
- The date you purchased the property and how much.
- The names on the property title.
- The receipts for the costs of renovations, maintenance and repairs.
- Details of interest charged on the property and rental income statements.

Selling a rental property- the process.

You can rent your property while selling it, if the tenants agree to stay in the house. The best way to do this is to reduce the rent of the property to compensate for the loss of privacy. Inform your property manager to put your property on the market. They will take care of everything. You can negotiate the real estate commission fee if they were managing your property while it was being rented out. If it is a rental, the agent will take care of all the issues dealing with the tenant in regards to open house. When someone put an offer on the house, the agent will contact you and fax (preferably) the document for you to accept or reject the offer. You can counter-offer and this process can go on until one party gives up (the offer is removed) and the property is again on the market. If the seller accepts the buyer's offer, they will both have to agree to that price in writing and must sign the acceptance form. This normally comes with the relevant clauses, such as subject to finance (30 days waiting period), which can be extended if the finance hasn't been approved.

If all is clear, then you can approach a settlement agent who will intercede on your behalf to complete the transaction. They will do all the paperwork and get you to sign the relevant form. Your settlement agent will attend settlement for you, pay the outstanding shire, amenity bills and put the balance of money into your account. The settlement agent smooth out the selling, legal and property ownership transfer for you.

Property settlement process:

1. Contracts: the seller's agent prepares a contract document about the property to be sold. The contract will include things like a copy of property title, any restrictive covenant, shared driveways, council zoning, usage status and planning permissions. These are forwarded to the buyer's settlement agent. The contract also states the settlement period of 30, 60 or 90 days and any special conditions required by the vendor such as building inspection.

2. Certificate of title: the vendor's solicitor or lawyer will search and obtain a certificate of title on the land or property to confirm the ownership. The search will check to see if there is any third party claim to the property, such as a finance company. It will also confirm the plan of the property, show where the property boundaries are, common land or private land.

3. Land transfer: you will sign on the land document to transfer the land or property to your name officially but not dated. This will be dated at settlement by your settlement agent when he/she lodges and pays the stamp duty on the value of the land or the house.

4. Body corporate: if it is a body corporate (villas, units) then your solicitor will check to confirm the details of the property, common area and any other issues related to the property.

5. Mortgage: your settlement agent will supply to the lender all documentation related to the contract of sale, the title search, insurance certificate and other applicable utility papers. Your bank will forward your mortgage documents to your settlement agent for you to sign off.

6. Extra fees and bills to be paid: your settlement agent will bring any bills up-to-date at settlement.

Records to keep:

- Records of real estate and settlement agents, accounting and advertising fees.
- Insurance fees.

- Shire, water rates and land tax bills.
- Paperwork on the sale of the property.
- Purchase paper and the names on the property title.
- The receipts for the costs of renovations, maintenance and repairs if applicable.
- Details of interest charged on the property and rental income statements.

Avoid selling your property if you can.

When your intention is property accumulation, it is wise to avoid selling any property. Selling a property unless it is really urgent should be avoided. Some people want a quick profit but forget that the short term profits will not last long. If you do this, there will nothing to show for your effort except receipts. Constantly buying and selling property is costly and time wasting. Around 10-15% of the profits will be eaten up in real estate agents fees (around 4% of the property price), stamp duty, settlement agent fees, plus capital gains tax.

Conclusion:

I hope that you've found the book informative and interesting. Remember over the long-term, property investors will always come up on top if you've followed all the advice outlined in the book. When I started investing, I did everything that I read in property investment magazines. However, I hit a minefield when interest rates started rising and I didn't fix my interest rate. I quickly learnt from my mistakes.

One lesson you need to learn is to fix your interest rates for at least five years if you're comfortable with the repayment. Always avoid expensive properties even if your tax deduction can cover the shortfall and there is good capital growth. It is better to have two cheaper properties than one expensive one. A cheaper property can become cash positive within a short time than an expensive one. When interest rates rise, an expensive property can quickly become an expensive asset and a burden. It can also lose value faster in a downturn than an average house. You can add value more easily on an average home than an expensive one.

You need to realise that not all properties are good investments. You cannot continue to accumulate negatively geared property even if your tax rate and deductions cover all the shortfalls. You will expect your investments to start to make some money sooner than later. A combination of negatively geared and positively geared properties is more viable than only negatively or only positively geared properties. You should aim for all your properties to become positively geared with capital growth over time (about 5-7 years), once you accumulated all your investments.

To order other copies of my books visit:
www.xlibris.com.au/Radegonde.html
www.stores.lulu.com/w478040
www.strategicpublishinggroup.com/title/PropertyInvestmentGuideforSuccessfulWealthCreationAndEarlyRetirement.html
wwww.tiny.cc/321qp
www.tiny.cc/JwJus- Upcoming and revised edition of the new book "Property Investment In Tough Times"

Common property words:

Appraisal/valuation: a written report of the estimated value of a property usually prepared by a qualified valuer.

Capital gain: the amount by which a property has increased compared to what you paid for. For example, you bought a property for $300,000 two years ago. It is worth $400,000. You've made a gross capital gain of $100,000.

CGT (capital gains tax): this is the tax you pay when you sell your property.

Cross-securitising/cross-collateralising: when the lender uses your property as security for other property you purchase.

Equity: the difference between your debt and what the property is worth. For example, your debt is $300,000 and the property is worth $380,000. You have $80,000 worth of equity in the property.

Interest only: only paying the interest charged on a loan/mortgage and not paying any of the principal (loan amount).

LMI (Lender's mortgage insurance): usually paid by the borrower to protect the lender against mortgage default when you borrow more than 80% of the property value.

Line of credit: a facility available that gives you an approved credit limit that you can draw down at any time.

Low-doc/no-doc loans: relatively new, these loans designed for self-employed people that require less documentation compared to a traditional loan.

Negative gearing: this is where the outgoings are more than rental income and all tax deductions. For example, if your rental income is

$900 per month and interest repayment is $1,500 per month; your shortfall is $600 which you can claim on your tax return.

Positive gearing: this occurs when the rental income on the investment exceeds interest repayments and all tax deductions. You might have to pay tax on the surplus income.

PPOR: principal place of residence: the house you live in.

Property cycle: property values follow a cycle of growth, a slowdown, a bust and an upturn. History shows that this occurs every 7 to 10 years.

LVR (loan to value ratio): to calculate this, divide the loan amount by the value of the property then multiply this sum by 100 to get a percentage. Financial institutions use this to determine if you can or cannot afford the loan repayment.

Split facility: allows you to lock part of your loan into a fixed interest rate for repayment certainty while at the same time leaving the other part of the loan variable and access to other features such as offset or withdraw facility.

Serviceability: if you can afford to pay the loan repayment, based on your income and expenses.

Redraw facility: this enables you to access any additional repayments are you need the cash.

Working out loan repayment is simple and important in investment: interest rate X loan amount in thousands For example, a $300,000 loan with a 6.75% interest rate, loan repayment: 300 (amount of loan in thousands) X 6.75=.

References and suggested readings.

Australian Property Investor. **Where to buy in 2007**. January 2007. www.apimagazine.com.au

Australian Property Investor. **How to find property hotspots before they Boom.** October 2006. www.apimagazine.com.au

Australian Property Investor Magazine. **Unlock High Returns.** August 2006.www.apimagazine.com.au

"Used by permission of Your Mortgage Magazine. www.yourmortgage.com.au . Copyright: Key Media, 2001-2009."

Information originally cited in Your Investment Property magazine. Edition 20.

22 Rising suburbs. March 2009.www.yipmag.com.au. Copyright: 2009 Key Media P/L.

Successful Real Estate & Property Investment For New investors: how to achieve financial freedom. Revised Edition.

Successful Real Estate & Property Investment For New investors: how to achieve financial freedom. Revised Edition.

www.ingramcontent.com/pod-product-compliance
Ingram Content Group UK Ltd.
Pitfield, Milton Keynes, MK11 3LW, UK
UKHW020119200726
13856UKWH00002B/637